KU-418-476

GLOBETROTTER

TRAVEL GUIDE

TANZANIA

GRAHAM MERCER

NEW
HOLLAND

GLOBETROTTER

TRAVEL GUIDE

*** Highly recommended
 ** Recommended
  * See if you can

First edition published in 1996
by New Holland (Publishers) Ltd
London • Cape Town • Sydney • Singapore

Reprinted 1997

24 Nutford Place
London W1H 6DQ
United Kingdom

80 McKenzie Street
Cape Town 8001
South Africa

3/2 Aquatic Drive
Frenchs Forest, NSW 2086
Australia

Copyright © 1996 in text: Graham Mercer
Copyright © 1996 in maps: Globetrotter Travel Maps
Copyright © 1996 in photographs:
Individual photographers as credited
Copyright © 1996 New Holland (Publishers) Ltd

All rights reserved. No part of this publication
may be reproduced, stored in a retrieval system
or transmitted, in any form or by any means,
electronic, mechanical, photocopying, recording
or otherwise, without the prior written permission
of the publishers and copyright holders.

ISBN 1 85368 424 4

Managing Editor: Sean Fraser
Editor: Donald Reid
Design and DTP: Sonya Cupido
Cartographer: William Smuts
Compiler/Verifier: Elaine Fick

Reproduction by cmyk prepress
Printed and bound in Hong Kong by Sing Cheong
Printing Co. Ltd.

Dedication:
To my father, who gave me my love of wildlife
and travel, and to my mother, who believed in me.

Acknowledgements:
I would like to thank Mohamed Amin, Ms. Patricia
Barrett, Ms Jamila Sumra, Ms Louise Whittle, all
the lovely people at Struik, the International School
of Tanganyika, my long-suffering safari partners
(Kevin Bartlett, Hamid Bharmal, John Boyce, Arshad
Hussain, Barry Whitemore and my wife Anjum)
and all the various rangers and game scouts of the
Tanzanian National Parks and Game Reserves.

Photographic Credits:
Peter Blackwell, all photographs except the
following: **Daryl and Sharna Balfour**, page 44;
Nigel J. Dennis, page 103; **Martin Edge**, pages
49–54; **Corrie Hansen**, page 118; **Peter Ribton**,
pages 19, 28, 31, 33, 35, 37, 38, 67.

Although every effort has been made to ensure
accuracy of facts, telephone and fax numbers in this
book, the publishers will not be held responsible for
changes that occur at the time of going to press.

Cover Photographs:
Top left: A *diving dhow rests up against a deserted
beach on Zanzibar.*
Top right: *The market place at Iringa, capital of the
Southern Highlands.*
Bottom left: *Camel safari in Arusha National Park,
beneath the volcanic slopes of Mt Meru.*
Bottom right: *A cheetah scans the endless grasslands
of Serengeti National Park.*
Title page: *Zebra in Ngorongoro Crater.*

CONTENTS

1
Introducing Tanzania

Tanzania is among the world's poorest countries, and at times among its most exasperating. For visitors it can often be expensive, hot, unsophisticated and exhausting. But there can be few, if any, countries in the world which are more exciting.

Its scenery alone, from the high snows of **Kilimanjaro** to the coral sands of **Zanzibar**, from the short-grass savanna to the petrified violence of the **Rift Valley**, is splendid. And yet these landscapes are little more than stages for a whole cast of wildlife spectaculars, including the greatest of natural double-acts, **Ngorongoro** and the **Serengeti**, scene of the annual migration which involves more than two million animals.

Less well-known but no less worthy of acclaim are sanctuaries such as **Lake Manyara**, famous for its flamingoes and tree-climbing lions, **Gombe Stream** with its chimpanzees, and those sleeping giants of the south, **Ruaha** and the **Selous**, elephant kingdoms extraordinary.

Tanzania's people, friendly and welcoming without being servile, range from Maasai pastoralists armed with spears to cosmopolitan city dwellers. Their history begins with man's first footsteps, printed in volcanic ash millions of years ago, and extends to the present day through the remarkable Swahili civilization, the slave trade, the Zanzibari sultanate and the great age of exploration, when men such as Livingstone and Stanley strode the land.

For those who can rise above its various challenges, Tanzania, the 'real Africa', awaits with an extended arm and a ready *Karibuni!* – 'Welcome!'

TOP ATTRACTIONS

*** Serengeti National Park: scene of the world's most astonishing animal migration.
*** Ngorongoro Crater: a Noah's Ark of animals shipwrecked in a volcanic bowl.
*** Zanzibar: historic island of slaves, sultans and spices.
*** Mount Kilimanjaro: highest and surely most symbolic mountain in Africa.
** Selous Game Reserve: one of the world's last and biggest wildernesses.
** Tarangire National Park: large herds of elephant and abundant wildlife.
** Lake Manyara: prolific bird life and striking scenery.

Opposite: *Ol Doinyo Lengai, in Tanzania's sector of the Rift Valley.*

THE GREAT RIFT VALLEY

● Visible from space, stretching from Jordan to the Zambezi, and more than 9700km (6000 miles) long, the Rift is Tanzania's main geographical feature.
● It has been formed by the intense underground stresses caused by shifts in the Earth's tectonic plates over a period of 20 million years. Even today there is turbulence below ground.
● For much of its length the valley is characterized by steep, sharply defined walls on both its eastern and western sides.
● Between the Danakil Depression in northern Ethiopia and Lake Tanganyika there are at least 30 active or semi-active volcanoes.

THE LAND

Tanzania measures 945,087 km² (364,898 sq miles) in area and contains the highest mountain in Africa, Kilimanjaro (5896m; 19,340ft), and part of its deepest lake, Tanganyika (358m; 1174ft). But statistics alone can convey nothing of the variety or attractiveness of Tanzania's topography, which ranges from mighty volcanic and ancient crystalline mountains to rolling tableland, from great lakes to seemingly endless grasslands, dense *miombo* woodland to palm-fringed coral sands.

The land is riven north to south by the eastern arm of the **Great Rift Valley**, the western fork of which, in the shape of Lake Tanganyika, helps to form Tanzania's western border. The country's eastern border is determined by the Indian Ocean, and in the south by the Ruvuma River. To the north the border with Kenya is more political than natural, except for a distinct kink around Kilimanjaro.

Mountains and Valleys

The best-known mountain in all Africa is surely **Kilimanjaro**, affectionately known as 'Kili'. Its familiar snow-capped dome rises regally from the Maasai plains in the north of the country. Close by is **Meru**, another beautiful volcanic mountain, and further west other orphans of violence proliferate in and around the Rift. Among them is Ol Doinyo Lengai, 'the Mountain of God' to the Maasai, and still active.

Below: *The dazzling snows of Kilimanjaro, only 3° south of the equator.*

Around Lengai the Rift is dramatic, with abrupt walls to east and west rising to between 270 and 680m (800 to 2000ft) above the floor. The sector of the Tanzanian Rift which most tourists cross, between Makuyuni and Lake Manyara, is less impressive as the eastern wall has eroded, though there are excellent views from the heights of the western wall. Beyond the Rift rise the **Crater Highlands**, including Ngorongoro, the most famous crater (more properly caldera) on Earth, and home to as many as 20,000 big game animals.

South of Kilimanjaro, the broken ranges of the **Eastern Arc** mountains ride south in craggy splendour. The light and cloud effects along these mountains, the **Pare** and the **Usambara**, can be spectacular. Further south the ranges swing inland to become the **Ulugurus** and **Udzungwas**, before merging into the **Southern Highlands**, a beautiful region centred around the small towns of Iringa and Mbeya. Southeast of Mbeya the **Livingstone Mountains**, named after the celebrated explorer, shelve with precipitous grandeur into the waters of Lake Malawi (a body of water still known as Lake Nyasa by many Tanzanians).

Above: *A typical first view of Ngorongoro, from the southern rim of the crater.*

TOURING TANZANIA

Despite its many attractions, Tanzania remains a very poor Third World country with an under-developed tourism sector. Simple things can take much longer than anticipated, and it is worth bearing in mind that a tour including Serengeti, Ngorongoro, Kilimanjaro and Zanzibar, the four principal attractions, will easily fill a fortnight. Visitors are advised to employ the services of a reputable tour company, arranged before or after arrival in Tanzania. Information on reputable tour companies and what they offer is given in the Travel Tips section at the back of the book.

Above: *The Rufiji River, life-blood of the mighty Selous Game Reserve.*

MONSTERS OF THE DEEP

Tanzania's inland waters can be huge and violent, as can some of the monsters living in them. Lake Victoria is the size of Scotland and Lake Tanganyika, almost deep enough to engulf five Eiffel Towers standing one on top of each other, is longer than Portugal. Both lakes are subject to fierce and sudden storms with 6m (20ft) swells, but beneath their surface live creatures equally daunting. The Nile Perch can exceed 227kg (500lb) and has been known to attack boats. A lungfish in Lake Victoria grows as long as 2m (7ft) and is quite capable of removing human fingers. Not surprisingly, stories of African equivalents to the Loch Ness monster are traded in the lakeside fishing communities.

The mountains and the Rift dominate their immediate landscapes, but the characteristic topography of Tanzania is the undulating **central plateau**, which averages 1200m (4000ft) above sea level. This tableland, which extends throughout much of the country, can be divided (roughly from northwest to southeast) according to its vegetation. In the northeast open grasslands and *Acacia-commiphora* woodland predominates, while in the south *miombo* woodland (mainly *Brachystegia* and *Julbernadia*) covers much of the landscape.

Inland Waters

Tanzania contains more surface water than any other African country. It is drained by a network of rivers, many of them seasonal, and along its western border lie the great lakes of **Victoria**, **Tanganyika** and **Malawi**. Victoria is the second largest and Tanganyika the second deepest lake in the world.

The largest river is the **Rufiji**, which drains a vast 177,400km² (68,500 sq miles) of land. Other significant rivers are the **Pangani**, which flows south from Kilimanjaro, the **Wami**, which waters two game areas, Mikumi and Saadani, and the **Ruvuma** river, which forms Tanzania's southern border with Mozambique. They all empty into the Indian Ocean.

Seas and Shores

The sea and and its fringes are an unexpectedly rich aspect of Tanzania, though 'dynamite fishing' and development are threatening their potential. The 800km (500 mile) coastline is typically tropical, with a coral reef and long stretches of white sand, often backed by groves of coconut palm or stands of feathery casuarina. Here and there this congruity of sea and sand is broken by estuaries or mangrove swamps, and in places low limestone cliffs and sea caves.

Fascinating ruins at **Kilwa** and on **Zanzibar** tell of the coast's history, while **Bagamoyo**, just opposite Zanzibar, became prominent as a mainland terminus of both the slave and ivory trade and the exploration of the interior. It lost its status when the Germans, recognizing the excellent natural harbour at **Dar es Salaam**, moved their administrative headquarters south in 1891.

Zanzibar lies low on the horizon opposite Bagamoyo, and often in cloud, as if ashamed of its somewhat murky past. Nowadays, however, both Zanzibar and **Pemba** (to the north) are engaged in more innocent business, bringing in boatloads of tourists rather than slaves. A similar emphasis also inspires **Mafia Island**, which is further south and known for its big game fishing, snorkelling and diving.

Below: *Secluded sands and exposed coral at Matemwe, on Zanzibar's northeast coast.*

SHORT RAINS, LONG RAINS

On the equator, the sun passes its zenith twice a year. Because of the phenomenon known as the intertropical convergence zone, about four weeks later the northeast and southwest trade winds converge, causing torrential rainfall typical of the tropics. Generally speaking, the **Short Rains** (mid-October to mid-December) are lighter and much less predictable than the **Long Rains** (mid-March to mid-May). Even during the long rains there can be dry and sunny days in most areas, though visitors can assume that April, throughout East Africa, will be pretty wet.

Climate

The climate of much of Tanzania is dictated by the two seasonal Indian Ocean trade winds, or monsoons, though across the country there are many local variations, mainly due to altitude differences and by the presence, in the west, of large bodies of surface water.

The northeast trades (*kasikazi* in Kiswahili) blow from late December to the beginning of March, bringing the **Short Rains**, the less welcome heat of the Arabian Gulf, and a sometimes oppressive sultriness to the coastal regions. On its tail, from approximately mid-March to mid-May, come the **Long Rains**, *mwaka*. The southeast trades, which generally blow from May to the end of September, curve in from the southern oceans, bringing pleasantly cooler, less humid air across the coast and far inland. Its arrival marks the beginning of the five- or six-month **dry season**, when plant growth, especially away from the coast, comes to a standstill and many watercourses cease to flow.

Because of the country's varied topography, the climate of Tanzania is not as predictable as tropical climates often are. Rain might fall, or fail to fall, when least expected, and the two distinct rainy seasons, characteristic of equatorial regions, will sometimes merge into one or vary considerably in length and intensity. On the whole, however, visitors to northern Tanzania can expect to find dry weather between June and the end of October, and a shorter dry spell from early January to mid-March. Further south the two rainy spells might not be so distinct, with variable precipitation likely from mid-November through to about mid-March.

Opposite: *Flat-topped acacia give attractive definition to the grasslands of Serengeti National Park.*

COMPARATIVE CLIMATE CHART	NGORONGORO				ZANZIBAR				IRINGA			
	SUM	AUT	WIN	SPR	SUM	AUT	WIN	SPR	SUM	AUT	WIN	SPR
	JAN	APR	JULY	OCT	JAN	APR	JULY	OCT	JAN	APR	JULY	OCT
AVE TEMP. °F	70	66	64	70	81	79	66	79	70	68	66	72
AVE TEMP. °C	21	19	18	21	27	26	19	26	21	20	19	22
SEA TEMP. °F	n/a	n/a	n/a	n/a	79	84	81	77	n/a	n/a	n/a	n/a
SEA TEMP. °C	n/a	n/a	n/a	n/a	26	29	27	25	n/a	n/a	n/a	n/a
HOURS SUN	8	6	7	8	8	6	8	8	7	8	10	9
DAYS OF RAINFALL	10	13	2	8	8	12	6	11	13	4	0	5
RAINFALL mm	99	114	9	74	94	232	46	155	128	25	1	63

Temperatures are also changeable, ranging from an average day-time figure of 30°C (86°F) at the coast, where the humidity is often high, to Arctic temperatures at the summit of Kilimanjaro. They vary seasonally as well, and visitors can generally expect cooler weather from mid-May to mid-November, particularly between early evening and mid-morning, though the sun can still be searingly hot at the height of the day. But even at the hottest times, cooling breezes or showers of rain can help to make life more tolerable.

Plant Life

In keeping with the variations in Tanzania's topography and climate, the country's plant life is richly diverse in form and distribution. Along the coast, **coconuts**, **casuarinas** and **mangroves** are common. Small (and sadly diminishing) remnants of coastal forest occur in patches a little way inland from the shoreline.

Further inland the natural tree cover in the southwestern half of the country is **miombo**, which gives way in the north to the open parkland of flat-topped **acacia** and 'apple orchard' **commiphora**, which so many people associate with East Africa. Undulating seas of grass make up large areas of the Serengeti, the Rift Valley and the plains below Kilimanjaro and Meru. These and other mountains are partly clothed in **montane forest**, and Kilimanjaro's altitude produces bands of fascinating and sometimes indigenous species of flora, including the **giant heathers** along the upper fringes of the rainforest, and the **giant lobelias** and **groundsels** of the alpine moorland zone.

Elsewhere in the country, where conditions are suitable, the **baobab** grows in corpulent and sometimes archaic grandeur, in places forming magnificent forests. And along the watercourses **figs**, **tamarinds** and **palms** add a welcome touch of green to the dessicated bush, even at the height of the dry season.

Wild flowers do not grow in great profusion, but there is a wealth of species, and when the rains come the bush can hum with vitality and colour. Some

---

EXOTIC BLOSSOMS

The trees and shrubs in Tanzania's towns are as cosmopolitan as the human population. Commonly seen species include:
● Jacaranda, Pride of Bolivia, and bouganvillea, all from South America.
● Flamboyant, the 'Zanzibar Christmas Tree', from Madagascar.
● Various species of hibiscus, originally from China.
● Pride of Barbados, and Indian almond, which speak for themselves.
● Bottlebrush and Australian flame, both from Australasia. These 'ex-pats' look beautiful and provide welcome shade, but they would struggle to survive alongside the thorny acacias and sinewy figs out in the 'real' world of the bush.

SWISS ARMY KNIFE OF THE PLANT KINGDOM

The coconut palm is not only very common, it is extremely versatile as well. A few of its functions are:
• as a takeaway meal and beverage in strong, disposable and environmentally friendly containers;
• the beginnings of a potent toddy, known as *tembo*, or elephant, and drunk in many coastal regions of Tanzania;
• oil for cooking or hair care, and in the manufacture of margarine, soap and candles;
• fibres for making string, rope and mats;
• fronds for thatching;
• an attractively grained timber used for making ornamental artefacts.

species are unique, such as the endangered African violets, and Kilimanjaro's *Impatiens kilimanjari*, an endemic red and yellow varietal of 'busy Lizzie'.

Cultivated plants include coffee, tea, cashew nuts, cloves, sugar and sisal, all important to Tanzania's economy. Maize, wheat, millet, sorghum, cassava, and rice are grown for home consumption, together with bananas and mangoes. A wide variety of vegetables and fruits come from the fertile central and northern regions of Kilimanjaro, Lushoto, Morogoro and Iringa.

Wildlife

There are many reasons for coming to Tanzania, but the main attraction is undoubtedly the country's wildlife and the magnificent habitats in which it is found. An astonishing 25% of Tanzania's land area is given over to protected wildlife zones, and 20% of Africa's larger mammals are to be found within the country. A dozen or more of these, often including one or two **big cats**, **elephant**, **buffalo**, **hippo**, **giraffe** and several **antelope** or **gazelle** can easily be seen in a brief trip to most national parks. Safari guides, on popular tours to the northern parks, feel disappointed if they haven't shown their clients 30 different kinds of

four-legged animals, from the **Big Five** down to hyrax and mongooses. The Big Five as the old hunters knew them – lion, leopard, elephant, buffalo and rhino - are found in most of Tanzania's parks and reserves, though leopard are not easily observed and the rhino have, in most places, either been killed off or exist in small numbers. **Cheetah** can usually be seen in the Serengeti (they occur elsewhere but not in such numbers) and rhino in Ngorongoro Crater. There are also **reptiles** such as crocodiles, monitor lizards and perhaps the odd snake. Keen birders, assuming they visit several parks and are accompanied by a knowledgeable guide, can expect to tick off well over 100 species (more than 1000 bird species are listed for Tanzania).

It should not be forgotten that Tanzania has Serengetis of the sea as well as the land. The Indian Ocean is rich in fascinating marine mammals, fish and reptiles, and Lake Tanganyika is full of endemic creatures. The rare and endangered **dugong**, several **turtles** and a whole host of **whales**, **dolphins**, **sharks** and **tropical fish** are found around and beyond the coral gardens of the coastal reefs.

Above: *Lady killers in Serengeti National Park.*

Conservation in Tanzania

Having a goose that lays golden eggs is one thing; taking care of the goose is another. Tanzania has an admirable record for creating wildlife sanctuaries, but its reputation for conserving them, as with so many other poor countries, has not always been so good. The decade following 1977 was particularly disastrous, with rhinos slaughtered almost to extinction and elephant populations devastated. The poachers were responding to demand, with horn and ivory fetching huge prices in Yemen, Taiwan, Hong Kong, India, China and elsewhere. Most of the carved ivory, interestingly, wound up in the west.

Control of poaching was hindered by poor morale and conditions among wardens, rangers and game scouts, lack of money and resources, poor management, widespread corruption, and by the flood of firearms following the war against Idi Amin in the late 1970s. It must be said, however, that many of the National Parks and Game Department personnel not only resisted the temptation to make easy money but did an excellent and often dangerous job in limiting the poaching menace.

THE MAGNIFICENT SEVEN

Where you can spot them:
- **Lion:** widespread, even outside the parks. *Almost* guaranteed in Serengeti and Ngorongoro, and usually seen in Tarangire, Manyara and Mikumi.
- **Leopard:** widespread but never guaranteed. Best chances are at Seronera Valley (Serengeti), Tarangire and Mikumi.
- **Cheetah:** often seen in the southern Serengeti, on the plains around Ngorongoro, and less often in Tarangire, Ruaha, and Selous.
- **Wild Dog:** much endangered, with unpredictable movements. Likeliest places are Mikumi, Selous, Serengeti and around Lake Ndutu.
- **Rhino:** Ngorongoro crater.
- **Elephant:** Serengeti, Ngorongoro, Manyara, Tarangire, Mikumi, Ruaha and Selous.
- **Chimpanzee:** Gombe Stream, Mahale Mountains.

Thanks to such people, the involvement of the Tanzanian Army, the pressure of world opinion, the support of wildlife organisations and the law of diminishing returns, serious poaching has been largely eliminated. There is still a lot of casual poaching, mostly 'for the pot', and it will be some time before the parks and reserves return to their pre-1970s best, but for the time being poaching is not the threat that it was.

There are other concerns. The greatest of these is the expanding population and its need for land and sustenance. Huge areas of land are being deforested, mostly to provide charcoal for cooking or a great deal of money for dealers in tropical hardwoods. Irresponsible and often illegal hunting is taking place in certain areas, often with the connivance of corrupt officials, leaving many animals indiscriminately killed or maimed. Increasing cultivation is reducing the habitat of wild animals outside (and sometimes inside) the strictly protected zones. Mangrove swamps and coral reefs, and the marine life which depends upon them, are being destroyed, often by fishermen using dynamite. And in at least one national park, Kilimanjaro, the popular trail to the summit is becoming degraded and littered through over-use.

The authorities concerned are aware of these problems and, with the help of outside organizations and individual benefactors, are trying hard to put things right. It will take time and money, and Tanzania alone cannot be expected to cope. Those privileged to enjoy Tanzania's wildlife sanctuaries are already helping by paying for their pleasures, a contribution it can only be hoped will be for the good of all concerned.

GOING UP IN SMOKE

One of the biggest conservation problems in Tanzania is deforestation, and one of its biggest causes is charcoal burning. Sacks of charcoal can often be seen along roadsides awaiting buyers. Most of it goes to Dar es Salaam or other urban areas, where consumption is high. It is the cheapest form of energy for cooking, which is mostly done on simple cooking stoves (*jikos*).

The charcoal burners of the bush belong to an ancient line of craftsmen, but their fascinating skills were once practiced in less populous times, causing little lasting destruction. But it takes 10 tonnes of raw wood to produce one tonne of charcoal, and today Tanzania's woodland is disappearing at a rate of up to 400,000ha (1500 sq miles) a year.

HISTORY IN BRIEF

East Africa has been called the 'Cradle of Mankind', though this distinction must presently rest with Ethiopia, where hominid remains dating back 4.4 million years have recently been discovered. Nevertheless, Tanzania's Olduvai Gorge, in the Ngorongoro Conservation Unit, has provided us with Nutcracker Man (*Australopithacus boisei*) and Handy Man (*Homo habilis*), both about 1.8 million years old, and, at the time of their discovery, significant landmarks in the study of man's past. In 1978 at Laetoli, just south of Olduvai, Mary Leakey found footprints of three upright-standing hominids in compacted volcanic ash, which had powdered the plains 3.7 million years ago.

More recently the aboriginal inhabitants of present-day Tanzania were hunter-gatherers. Other tribes gradually moved in, seeking better land and displacing or absorbing the aborigines. The newcomers were Bantu, entering from the regions between the western lakes. By AD1300 they had spread into the areas of heavy rainfall, leaving the plains to the Nilo-Hamitic pastoralists who came down later from the north.

Arrival of the Arabs

The first non-Africans to visit the area were probably **traders** from Arabia, Persia and India, who eventually settled along the coast with the aim of taking better advantage of trading opportunities or simply because the fertile, relatively peaceful coastal strip was preferable to conditions at home. Being dependent upon the monsoons they would have been obliged, in any case, to stay in East Africa for months at a time.

This settlement of the 'Land of Zinj' (Land of Blacks) began with **Arab** immigrants in about AD800, who were joined 400 years later by **Shirazis** (originally from Persia). Intermarriage between these newcomers and local

---

DHOWS

As late as 1946, 678 foreign dhows came into Zanzibar, a total probably unsurpassed in East African history. But the large and beautiful *bagh-lahs* and *booms* (the word 'dhow' is generic and there are many specific types) have become extinct, or are almost so. *Jahazis* of over 9m (30ft) can still be seen, along with smaller *daus* and *mashuas*, the outrigger *ngalawas* and the dug-out *mtumbwis*. Dhows ply the Zanzibar Channel, carrying anything from cloves or cement to chicken feed or corrugated iron, yet few craft evoke the romance of the eastern seas more strongly, leaning into a marbled blue sea, its lateen sail stretched into graceful curves by a steady monsoon.

Opposite: *A game drive through the northern sector of the Selous Game Reserve.*
Below: *All our yesterdays; relics of early man in Olduvai Gorge museum.*

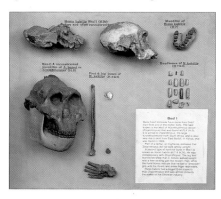

Above: *The symbols of Stone Town: a Swahili girl, wearing a* **kanga**, *stands by an ornate Zanzibar door.*
Opposite: *Caves used to hide slaves after the trade was abolished in 1873 at Mangapwani on Zanzibar.*

Africans produced the **Swahili** people who soon established a rich and enterprising civilization. The resulting language, Kiswahili, is now spoken throughout East Africa.

Arab and African lifestyles effectively fused into the common Swahili culture, and by the 15th century 37 Swahili towns existed in Zinj. Despite constant bickering among these tiny 'city states', commerce flourished until 1498, when the arrival of Portuguese navigator **Vasco da Gama**, stopping off from his remarkable passage to India, signalled a new era.

The Portuguese Centuries

Da Gama, and the compatriots who followed in his wake two years later, were not interested in colonizing Zinj, and made little effort to explore the interior. The Portuguese who found themselves on the Swahili coast were guardians rather than settlers, maintaining bases from which ships could be provisioned and the safety of the shipping lanes between Portuguese territories in Muscat, Goa and Mozambique secured.

They were, however, well-armed and ruthless. By 1509 the Swahili towns, already disunited, were subdued, with

---

HISTORICAL CALENDAR

3.7 million years BC Three hominids leave their footprints at Laetoli, near Olduvai Gorge
750,000 years BC Volcanic Kilimanjaro formed.
AD800 Arab traders settle on East African coast.
AD1000 Bantu tribes moving in from west; on coast Swahili civilisation beginning.
1498 Arrival of navigator Vasco da Gama, followed by Portuguese rule along coast.
1600 British ships appearing in Indian Ocean.
1699 Omani Arabs seize East coast. Portuguese retreat.

1800 Maasai spreading southwards into northern Tanzania.
1832 Seyyid Said transfers seat of sultanate from Oman to Zanzibar. Era of prosperity for Zanzibar begins.
1860 John Speke leaves Zanzibar to find the source of the Nile.
1871 Stanley sets out from Zanzibar to find Livingstone.
1873 Livingstone dies. Zanzibar slave market closes.
1890 Anglo-German agreement. Mainland Tanzania becomes German East Africa, Zanzibar a British protectorate.
1914–18 World War I. After

fierce campaign in East Africa Britain takes control of what becomes known as Tanganyika.
1961 Tanganyika independent; Zanzibar follows in 1963.
1964 Revolution in Zanzibar. Sultan flees. Three months later Zanzibar and mainland brought together as United Republic of Tanzania.
1978 Idi Amin's Ugandan army invades western Tanzania. Repelled and defeated.
1985 President Nyerere steps down and is succeeded by Ali Hassan Mwinyi.
1995 First multi-party elections.

Kilwa and Mombasa reduced to rubble. For the next two centuries the Portuguese occupied the coast, but they were always insecure, threatened by Turkish pirates and later, at the beginning of the 17th century, by the appearance of an increasing number of British ships.

By 1729, with their Indian empire in disarray, the Portuguese were forced to flee by the **Omani Arabs**. The Omanis had raided Mombasa in 1660, and after the stronghold at Fort Jesus fell, the Portuguese sailed south to Mozambique, leaving little behind but bad feeling, rusting cannon, and a host of introduced crops, such as cassava, pineapples, pawpaws and groundnuts.

The Rule of Zanzibar

The Omani sultan, distracted by feuding and rivalries at home, had to leave his newly won East African possessions to various representatives. The Mazrui family, which had been given authority for Mombasa, took advantage of a change of leadership in Oman and declared an independent sheikdom, attacking other settlements. In response to pleas for help, the new sultan in Oman, **Seyyid Said**, sailed south, capturing Pemba in 1822. He was thwarted in his attempts to win back Mombasa, but he fell in love with Zanzibar, and in 1832 transferred the seat of his Imamate to the island. Said was the power behind Zanzibar's rise, establishing the clove industry that was to prove so profitable, and he was to hold considerable influence over events both along the coastal strip and deep into the interior. He also boosted the turnover of that more sordid business, the trade in human lives.

Slaving had gone on for at least 2000 years, but under the Zanzibar sultans it reached its awful peak. Up to 30,000 slaves a year were brought to Zanzibar in the early 1870s, to work the clove plantations or to be sold in the market. Great caravans left Bagamoyo for the interior, returning with slaves and ivory. Zanzibari traders made fortunes, and helped to depopulate huge areas.

> ### A MOVEABLE FEAST
>
> The Moroccan traveller, **Ibn Batuta**, visited the East African coast in 1331, and remarked that the people he found were 'very fat and corpulent'. Though the Swahilis enjoyed a rich diet, they couldn't compete in terms of protein sufficiency with the Zimba, another coastal people – with a taste for human flesh. When the Portuguese attacked the city states in Zinj, they enlisted the help of these cannibals, who literally ate their way from Kilwa to Malindi. They devoured dogs, lizards and rats, as well as the citizens of Kilwa and Mombasa. At Malindi the Portuguese, perhaps afraid of appearing on their menu, turned on the Zimba, almost wiping them out.

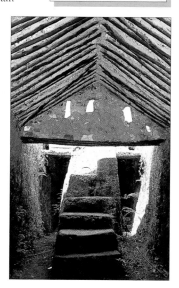

SULTAN SAID

Said succeeded to the Omani throne at the age of 15 by plunging a knife into the stomach of his cousin, the regent, and his first sight of the East African coast was at the head of an invading army. Yet Sultan Said saw himself as a merchant rather than a warrior king. It was his success in dealing with slaves, ivory and cloves that brought prosperity to Zanzibar, and earned him the title 'Said the Great'. A less well-known aspect of his enterprising spirit is that he sold another kind of spirit, brandy, to fellow Muslims. Nevertheless he was a surprisingly simple man, courteous and fair-minded, who in matters of justice was said to treat his own sons and the lowest of slaves as equals.

Below: *A crucifix made from the wood of the tree under which Livingstone's heart was buried in 1857.*

The Great Explorers and the Scramble for Africa

As slaves poured into Zanzibar during the third quarter of the 18th century, a succession of outstanding men were heading in the opposite direction. It was the age of the **explorers**, when the nagging question of the source of the Nile was eventually 'settled' (by John Speke) and when giants of exploration and evangelical zeal – Krapf, Burton, Livingstone, Stanley, Grant, Thomson, Von der Decken and Teleki – strode out on their 'long walks'.

All these explorers passed through Zanzibar, which had continued to prosper under successive sultans, although their power dwindled as the British exerted diplomatic and military authority. Under pressure, Sultan Barghash closed the slave market in Zanzibar in 1873, and soon afterwards, during the 'Scramble for Africa', the British made various treaties with Germany. They effectively took control in Zanzibar and much of what is now Kenya and Uganda, with most of present-day Tanzania, Rwanda and Burundi becoming known as **German East Africa**.

German rule was generally regarded as harsh. Its early years were marked by an Arab uprising along the coast, a war with the Hehe, and the Maji-Maji rebellion of 1905, in which the whole southern region united against their German overlords. All revolt was savagely suppressed, but the backlash against the Maji-Maji rebellion left the south devastated and 120,000 Africans dead. In Germany there was much disquiet about such brutality, although the Germans did do more to develop the country than their gentler successors, the British.

Tanganyika and Tanzania

In 1914 **World War I** came to East Africa. German-led forces, under their brilliant commander Von Lettow-Vorbeck, fell back before the British in a strategic retreat, keeping much-needed British manpower and resources from the Western Front until the end of the war. By the end of 1916, however, the British had established a provisional administration, and from 1922 the country, renamed Tanganyika, was governed by them under a

Left: *A crumbling former Sultan's Palace (and now a museum) in Stone Town, Zanzibar Island.*

League of Nations mandate. Zanzibar, Pemba and the coastal strip, however, remained in the possession of the Zanzibar sultanate.

By and large the British regarded Tanganyika as a poor relation of neighbouring Kenya. Soon after World War II, which had little direct impact on Tanganyika, the 'winds of change' began to blow and on 9 December 1961 the nation became independent, with **Julius Nyerere** at its head. Zanzibar's independence followed in December 1963 but a month later the last of its sultans was deposed in a bloody revolution. A few months after the revolution an arranged (and still troubled) marriage was convened between Zanzibar and Tanganyika, creating the United Republic of Tanzania.

At the crux of the new republic was socialism, and the radical concept of *ujamaa*, derived from the Chinese Communist system of a village-based economy. Though Nyerere remained popular, his policies were less so, as Tanzania slid into severe economic depression, exacerbated by the break up of the East African Economic Community in 1977, and the war with Idi Amin's Uganda in 1978.

Nyerere stepped down as president in 1985. His successor, **Ali Hassan Mwinyi**, a Zanzibari, has helped to guide Tanzania towards a multi-party system, with elections first held in October 1995.

THE GREAT EXPLORERS

Tanzania was the hub of many of the well-known 19th-century explorations into 'Darkest Africa'. Most of them were remarkable rather than loveable.

● **David Livingstone**, called 'The Good One' by the Africans. A determined man, he often depended upon the hospitality of the slave traders he despised, and Stanley found him not preaching the Bible but instead searching ambitiously for the source of the Nile.

● **H.M. Stanley**, who presumed to meet Livingstone at Ujiji in western Tanzania, and subsequently became one of Africa's greatest explorers in his own right.

● **Richard Burton**, an incredible personality who was fluent in 29 languages, wrote 43 volumes about his exciting and often dangerous travels, and translated the famous *Arabian Nights*.

● Not to be forgotten are the African and Swahili pioneers. Among them was **Juma bin Rajabu**, who was trading in Unyamwezi in the 1840s when Ludwig Krapf, the first European to explore the interior, was still at a mission near Mombasa. He met Burton and Speke, introducing them to his 18-year-old son, who was to become notorious as the great slaver, **Tippu Tip**.

GOVERNMENT AND ECONOMY

From independence until October 1995 the Tanzanian Government was elected by universal suffrage under a single-party system. The original mainland and Zanzibar factions of the ruling party merged in 1977 to form the Revolutionary Party of Tanzania, Chama Cha Mapinduzi, or CCM as it is known. Elections were held every five years for the office of president and for the 300 seats in the National Assembly. The government was dedicated to the socialist ideas outlined in Nyerere's Arusha Declaration of 1967, and much influenced by Mao Tse-tung's China.

Under President Mwinyi, and pressure from the World Bank, the IMF and western governments, emphasis gradually shifted from extreme socialism to a more democratic election process, which has culminated in the introduction of a multi-party system.

Economy

Radical socialism, poor management, corruption, the collapse of the East African Economic Community, steeply rising oil prices and the brave but financially ruinous rout of Idi Amin, all contributed to Tanzania's economic collapse during the 1970s. Tanzania had always been poor, and the infrastructure inherited from the British was limited, but by the late 1970s Nyerere's much-vaunted policy of 'self-reliance' became a cruel joke, as Tanzania rattled the begging bowl from east to west.

In the mid-1980s pressures for change began to take effect, with a gradual liberalization of the economy. The Tanzanian shilling was drastically devalued and is now pegged to the dollar, inefficient parastatals and nationalized companies were handed over to private ownership, import restrictions and currency regulations were eased and foreign investment encouraged. By the late 1980s, thanks to Tanzania's compliance with western demands, it became the second-largest recipient of non-military aid in the world.

MWALIMU

Julius Nyerere was educated at a mission school near Lake Victoria, then went on to university in Uganda and Scotland. He became involved in politics on his return to Tanzania, and was at the forefront of movements towards independence. In 1961 he became Prime Minister of the new nation of Tanganyika, establishing his policy of *ujamaa*. Revered as the 'Father of the Nation', and widely known as *Mwalimu*, or teacher, many see him as a failed idealist. Tanzania's economy collapsed disastrously during his rule, but he did bestow some of his personal dignity upon his country and its people. He was a vocal opponent of repression in South Africa and elsewhere, and under him Tanzania, in a continent ravaged by war and tribalism, remained stable and peaceful. He remains a widely respected elder statesman.

But genuine recovery will be slow and (for most people) painful. Extreme socialism left Tanzania destitute, but 'liberalization', whatever its long-term benefits, has coincided with an increase in unemployment, crime and corruption. These problems are exacerbated by the inefficiencies and frustrations of a country conditioned to state control, by extensive power cuts which are damaging businesses and industrial output, and by a disturbing increase in drug trafficking, drug abuse and AIDS.

The country remains among the poorest in the world, and yet some outside investment is being attracted, the promising tourist industry is being overhauled, shops are relatively well-stocked and buildings such as hotels, restaurants and banks are going up in Dar es Salaam and elsewhere. This doesn't help the Tanzanian masses who somehow scrape by on astonishingly low salaries; in real terms they are worse off than they were under Nyerere. Prices are rising, inflation stands at around 40%, and the great imbalance between rich and poor is widening. But there is hope, even optimism in many quarters. Much depends upon the pace and extent of any 'filter-down effect', and the remarkable patience of the ordinary Tanzanians.

Natural Resources

Despite its poverty Tanzania is a country of abundant natural resources, including gemstones, gold, gypsum, fossil fuels and the many outstanding tourist attractions. Among its cash crops are coffee, tea, cotton, sisal, tobacco, cloves, cashew nuts and pyrethrum. This vital agricultural sector, neglected for years because of falls in world demand and lack of incentives within the country, is beginning to recover.

TANZANIA IN NUMBERS

- **Population** (1995 est.): 28 million.
- **Birth rate** per 1000 population: 50.5 (world ave. 27.1)
- **Death rate** per 1000 population: 14.0 (world ave. 9.9)
- **Life expectancy:** male 51.3 years; female 54.7 years.
- **Enrolment at primary school** as a % of total school-age population: 50%
- **Enrolment at secondary school** as a % of total school-age population: 5%.
- **Principal exports:** coffee beans 20.2%; raw cotton 18.7%; tobacco 3.2%; cloves 1.7%; tea 1.5%.

Opposite: *Ali Hassan Mwinyi, President of Tanzania from 1985 to 1995.*

Below: *The fertile, sweeping upland and mountain areas which characterize Tanzania's Southern Highlands.*

PLANES, TRAINS...

● A few years ago Tanzania's major **highways** looked like the aftermath of the Battle of the Somme, but now many roads, including the link from Dar to the north, and much of the Tanzam highway between Dar and the Zambian border, have been resurfaced.
● The **rail** network, especially along the Uhuru Railway, built by the Chinese between Dar and Zambia, is also being upgraded, though journeys can still be long. There are three classes of travel.
● **Air Tanzania** has internal links between a number of towns. There are two types of fare, resident and non-resident; the latter has to be paid in US$.
● **Ferries** are an important aspect of Tanzania's transportation, with services to Zanzibar, Pemba, Mafia, and around the great lakes.

Below: *A hydrofoil ferry approaches Zanzibar.*
Opposite: *Maasai elders in the Rift Valley.*

Health and Education

Health care is rudimentary in Tanzania. There are **hospitals** in all the major towns, but they are mostly poorly equipped, with their staff often demoralized, though the best Tanzanian doctors have an excellent reputation. Small towns and villages usually have clinics, but these again are usually bereft of all but the simplest medical facilities.

Schools are similarly poor, in terms of resources (many have no desks or writing materials) and academic performance. Teachers are often not paid for months on end, and attendance, among teachers and students alike, can be very erratic. Some successful students manage to win overseas scholarships, while others have the opportunity to attend university in Dar es Salaam. However, opportunities for graduates who remain in the country are limited, and remuneration is pathetically low.

Tourism

At the end of the 1970s, when the border with Kenya was closed following the break-up of the East African Economic Community, it was not unknown for a tourist or expatriate to have whole national parks more or less to themselves, sometimes for days on end.

Although it is still possible, in the southern parks, to spend whole mornings or evenings without encountering another vehicle, increasingly the tourist industry is becoming aware of the enormous potential. Large numbers of **safari companies** are now operating, mostly from Arusha and specializing in tours to the well-known northern parks. **Hotels** and **lodges** are being built wherever tourism looks likely to succeed, and a big effort is being made to improve, especially by offering standards of accommodation and service that will make tourists both comfortable and appreciated.

THE PEOPLE

There are about 26 million Tanzanians, from approximately 120 tribes. No tribe is dominant and this, together with the Tanzanians' easy-going and tolerant nature, has ensured relative racial harmony throughout the country since independence. The policies of former president Julius Nyerere, who added 'factionalism' to the list of evils to be eradicated by his government, also helped.

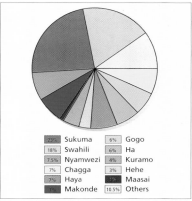

23%	Sukuma	6%	Gogo
18%	Swahili	6%	Ha
7.5%	Nyamwezi	4%	Kuramo
7%	Chagga	3%	Hehe
7%	Haya	7%	Maasai
7%	Makonde	10.5%	Others

THE TRIBAL GROUPS OF TANZANIA

This is not to say that racial problems do not exist; Tanzanians of one tribe will often criticize another, but not usually with malice. The most worrying trend is the growing resentment towards the **Asian** communities, who are seen by many Tanzanians as exploitative and corrupt. Though they remain watchful rather than panicky, should they leave, their loss would be sadly detrimental to Tanzania's economy and cultural diversity.

Tribes

Everyone in the world, it seems, knows the **Maasai**, those rather over-exposed (in more senses than one) and colourful pastoralists that seem to figure on the cover of so many books about East Africa. They are a striking and fascinating people, and the fact that many of them now work in offices, handling computers and wearing smart western-style clothes does not detract from the tribe's enduring, if much romanticized, allure. Members of the Barabaig, the Gogo and the Hehe tribes are often mistaken by visitors for Maasai, as men often wear the loose-fitting blanket or cotton

Above: *A Swahili woman.*
Opposite: *A village near Lake Rukwa in southwestern Tanzania.*

wrap, and many of the women shave their heads and wear brightly coloured beaded necklaces and earrings.

West of Maasailand, between the Rift and Lake Victoria, lives another striking tribe of pastoralists of Bantu origin, the **Sukuma**. In past times their young warriors, like those of the Maasai, would prove their manhood by spearing a lion. In common with the Maasai and other tribes, their young men and women still endure the pain and (for them) the privilege of ritual circumcision.

An even fiercer warrior tribe, the **Barabaig**, is centred around Mount Hanang, on the edge of the Rift Valley in the northwest. To the south live the **Gogo**, the people seen in and around the central town of Dodoma. They, like the Barabaig, energetically resisted the Maasai during their 19th-century incursions. They are said to have suffered greatly during the 1914–18 period, when they got caught up in someone else's war, and later from Nyerere's enforced ujamaa policies. Unlike the Maasai the Gogo are Bantu, and cultivators.

Further south still, in the neighbourhood of the southern town of Iringa, are the **Hehe**, also feared in the past for their warlike disposition and their stand against the Maasai. They rebelled against the Germans during the colonial period and despite the heavy odds, taught the Europeans a few lessons in military strategy.

The Hehe had previously been threatened by the warlike **Ngoni**, an offshoot of the Zulu peoples who migrated north and settled around what is now the town of Songea, in southwest Tanzania. The Ngoni, after many pitched battles with the Hehe, were finally defeated in the decisive battle of Itambolo.

East of the Ngoni, who of course live peacefully now like all the other tribes, lives a tribe of woodcarvers, the **Makonde**, whose homeland straddles the border with Mozambique in the southeast coastal region. The coast and its hinterland is home to various tribes, but its ethnic flavour is **Swahili**. Traditional Swahili villages nestle among palms in the shade of mango trees, among small-holdings (*shambas*) of cashew, cassava, bananas or pawpaw. The huts are made of mud and wattle, thatched with *makuti* – grass or palm fronds (though now often corrugated iron).

In contrast, the traditional huts of the **Chagga**, the people of Kilimanjaro, were constructed of saplings thatched with grass, in the shape of an old-fashioned bee-hive. They too are disappearing, for the Chagga are a very enterprising and forward-looking race, much involved in business throughout the country. Tourists visiting Kilimanjaro will encounter the Chagga every-where, particularly if they opt to climb the mountain, as the tribe provides the porters and the guides.

Most of the other tribes (it is impossible to describe more than a few) are equally interesting, from the **Hadzapi** and **Sandawe** hunter-gatherers to the 'Children of the Moon', the **Nyamwezi**, across whose lands in central Tanzania the explorers had to travel to reach the Lakes.

Village Life

The life style of most Tanzanians is hard and limited, especially for women in the villages, who do much of the work as well as bearing and bringing up children. The birth rate is high and life expectancy low, although the latter is gradually improving. Villagers in particular spend much of their lives struggling to make ends meet; producing enough food (often with primitive tools), building huts, gathering fuel and fetching water. Life in the towns is, on the whole, seen as preferable (hence a gradual urban drift), though at the bottom of the pile beg-gars and street children lead a demeaning life.

> ### THE MEN OF MAASAI
>
> Traditional Maasai males:
> ● At the age of **four** or **five**, have two central lower incisors removed (to allow for feeding in case of lockjaw). They are given responsibility for the family's lambs, kids, and calves.
> ● At the age of **six**, have their upper ear lobes pierced. Given responsibility for slightly older animals.
> ● At **puberty**, expected to undergo circumcision without anaesthetic.
> ● After an interim period, become junior warriors *ilmurran*; live with younger girls and the girls' mothers in a *manyatta* (warrior camp).
> ● At about **20**, become senior warriors.
> ● At about **27**, they become junior elders, and are allowed to marry.
> ● In their **30s**, join ranks of senior elders.
> ● In **old age**, cared for as *desati*, retired elders.
> ● On **death**, are put out in bush to be eaten by hyenas etc. Only distinguished elders and *loibons* (Maasai prophets) are buried.

THE MAKONDE CARVERS

Many Makonde moved into Tanzania from northeast Mozambique to avoid the ravages of war. These proud and highly sensitive people tend to isolate themselves in small groups and are regarded by other tribes with respect and sometimes a superstitious fear. Men and women file their teeth to points and adorn their faces and bodies with elaborate citracising, and the women wear large lip plugs made of metal. Their tribal ceremonies involve dancing, twisting and spinning on very high stilts, but they are best known for their 'ebony' carvings (actually African blackwood). The best place to see these are at the Mwenge Handicraft Market, just to the north of Dar es Salaam. The best of these – often traditionally symbolic or abstracts of finely detailed family groups called *ujamaa* carvings – are unique, imaginative and quality works of art. There is, however, the usual mediocre stuff and 'touristy' souvenirs. Visitors should be prepared to take a long look around, and to haggle.

Religion

Many rural people are animist, but most Tanzanians are Christian or Muslim. The Muslims, mostly living along the coast and in Zanzibar, represent about one third of the population, the majority of the remaining two thirds being Christian. The small Asian communities are mostly made up of Hindus, Sikhs and Muslims.

Sport and Recreation

The sporting passion among men and boys is **soccer** (football). Favourite teams are fervently supported in the large towns, and even in the villages boys will be seen kicking around a ball made of rags. **Boxing** and **wrestling** enjoy a minority following among the men, with **darts** being common in many bars and clubs. **Netball** is popular with women, and **volleyball** is sometimes played by both sexes.

Water sports are not as popular with Tanzanians as one might expect in a country with a wonderful coastline and many lakes and rivers. Bilharzia (and sometimes hippos and crocodiles!) are a problem in freshwater lakes, though some people take at least an occasional dip in the sea.

Right: Bao, *a traditional game played with beans and a wooden board with cups scooped out of it, being played on Mafia island.*

Almost all Tanzanians love **music** and **dancing**, with Zairean rhythms and bands being especially popular. And they love **conversation** (often sexually segregated, with urban, non-Muslim menfolk chatting in bars or clubs over a few bottles of lager, and in the villages in the shade of some tree, perhaps with a home-made brew). Other than traditional music and dancing, there is little interest in the performing or visual arts.

Above: *Worshippers on Zanzibar gather for a musical celebration at a Tarab festival.*

Food and Drink

The **staple** food in most parts of Tanzania is *ugali* – a stiff maize or cassava porridge. Beans, *mchicha* (a form of spinach) and bananas are also popular. **Meat** is much too expensive for the majority of Tanzanians to eat regularly. When it is affordable it is often eaten in the form of *mishkaki*, small chunks of barbecued beef, or as a kind of stew with plantains, known as *nyama na ndizi*. Many Tanzanians enjoy a kind of deep-fried doughnut (*mandazi*) for breakfast. These are delicious with tea, which the Tanzanians prefer Indian fashion, boiled with milk and stiff with sugar.

WaZungu (western) food is regular fare in tourist lodges and hotels, though Tanzanian dishes are appearing more often on the menu, and delicious tropical fruits, including paw-paws, mangoes, bananas, pineapple and water melon are almost always served. Culinary standards vary but the food is generally adequate and, at its best, very acceptable. The English breakfast fights a rearguard action, and lunch and dinner is the traditional 'meat and two veg', sometimes masterfully overcooked in time-honoured tradition. Even 'pudding' survives, though the ubiquitous fruit salad has become the easy alternative.

Vegetarians are increasingly, though not always imaginatively, catered for in hotels and restaurants, and most towns offer the universal forms of fast food. **Street fare**, especially the kebab-like *mishkaki*, and *sekela* (barbecued) chicken, are a common, tasty, and normally safe alternative. In Dar (and to a lesser extent elsewhere) there is a whole range of national alternatives, including Chinese, Greek, Indian, Italian and Lebanese.

SEAFOOD

With one border on the Indian Ocean, lovers of seafood will find much to delight them in Tanzania. Lobsters, prawns and calamari are readily available in most good hotels along the coast, and fish such as red or blue snapper, rock cod, sole, changu, and kingfish all make excellent eating. Lobster, garlic prawns or prawns *pili pili* (with a hot and spicy sauce), and various barbecued dishes are among local favourites.

2
Dar es Salaam
and the Coast

Dar es Salaam is not particularly old or beautiful, but it is interesting and attractively situated. It has a disarming lack of pretension and its people, on the whole, are similarly casual and engaging, representing a colourful and cosmopolitan community.

Half-encircled by the waters of the **Indian Ocean**, Dar stands, or rather sleepily sprawls, mid-way down Tanzania's coastline. This coastal strip, 800km (500 miles) long, was once part of the medieval land of Zinj and the surprisingly advanced and enterprising Swahili civilization. It later became a fiefdom of the Zanzibari sultans, who sold it (under pressure) to the Germans during the 'Scramble for Africa'. The area is scattered with interesting ruins, such as those at **Kilwa**, formerly a famous and prosperous Swahili settlement. It is also a shoreline of some beauty, with many fine **beaches** and a sea teeming with fascinating marine life and, where the reefs have not been destroyed by 'dynamite fishing', ornamented with natural coral gardens.

Seventy kilometres (45 miles) north of Dar is **Bagamoyo**, whose clusters of Swahili huts and old buildings recall its 19th-century heyday when huge caravans bringing slaves and ivory from the interior, and explorers heading the other way, would pass through. Beyond Bagamoyo lies **Saadani Game Reserve**, where big game can be found alongside the sea, and further north still are the drowsily pleasant little towns of **Pangani** and **Tanga**.

CLIMATE

The coastal climate is generally hot and humid, with an average daytime temperature of 30°C (86°F). The hottest months are from November to February or March, but from June to October the southeast monsoon brings cooler, drier weather. From March to May the Long Rains bring heavy showers, but the rain rarely lasts all day, and may be alleviated by days, or even weeks, of intermittent sunshine.

Opposite: *Living palm and dying dhow; small symbols of a significant past on Bagamoyo beach.*

DON'T MISS

** **Strolling around Dar:**
especially Azania Front,
the harbour and the
National Museum.
** **Dar's beaches:** both
north of the city at Oyster
Bay and Kunduchi, and on
the southern shores.
** **Mwenge Handicraft
Market:** where you'll find the
famous Makonde carvings.
* **Bagamoyo:** the hub
of a historic coastline.
* **Kilwa:** fascinating
ancient ruins, though
getting there isn't simple.

DAR ES SALAAM

The inspiration behind Dar es Salaam was **Sultan
Majid**, ruler of Zanzibar, who in 1866 began to build
a palace on the mainland. His 'Haven of Peace' (as
Dar es Salaam is commonly translated) was to have
been his refuge from a troubled reign on the island,
but Majid died in 1870 before his dreams could be
fulfilled. His palace has gone, and all that remains
of Majid's dreams is a fortified building, the Old Boma,
on Sokoine Drive.

Seven years after Majid's death his 'Darra Salaam',
according to one report, 'teemed with snakes, scorpions,
centipedes, mosquitoes and other pests'. The **Germans**,
seeking a deep-water harbour, shifted their headquarters
down from Bagamoyo, and by 1914 they had built a railway from Dar to Lake Tanganyika. This proved good
timing for the British, who promptly took it over during
World War I. Appropriately, the hostilities hardly disturbed the Haven of Peace, though the Royal Navy did
lob a few shells shorewards, dislodging coconuts and
badly damaging the old State House.

Dar es Salaam under German rule was an organized
and pretty place. Even now Dar's shoreline is a pleasure

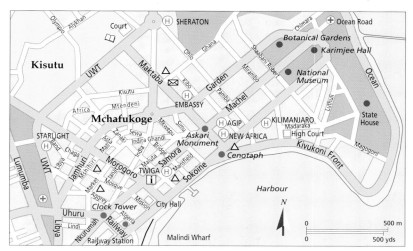

to drive along, with its fine harbour and the blue seas and white sands which sweep around the northern suburbs. Like the Germans, the **British** erected various civic buildings and amenities, as well as bungalows and houses surrounded by lawns and gardens, though bougainvillea and hibiscus tended to proliferate rather than the honeysuckle and roses of home.

Away from the immediate centre Dar is still a refreshingly 'green' city., but is becoming less so. Buildings are going up everywhere, many of them high-rise and purely functional, and road traffic has increased considerably in recent years. However, shops are fairly well stocked, and Dar es Salaam is beginning to reflect a more dynamic and forward-looking Tanzania.

City Centre **

Dar es Salaam is an absorbing, laid-back mixture of east and west, old and new, races, tribes, religions and political philosophies; an all-pervading, often endearing miscellany of mankind. The city can be dirty, hot, humid, exasperating, shallow and unsophisticated, but it is rarely boring, and most people who live there hold it in great affection. It is the country's main port and economic, cultural and political centre, and, until the move is made to Dodoma (anticipated around the turn of the century), the capital city.

SAFETY ON THE STREETS

In many ways the Haven of Peace is just that, and with common sense the visitor should enjoy an unmolested stay. Dar is no more threatening than most other big cities, but it has its share of thieves, pickpockets and con-men, and appropriate care should be taken.

● The coast is predominantly Muslim, and street clothes which are too revealing, while not exactly frowned upon in Dar itself, will sometimes attract unwelcome attention.

● The wearing of expensive-looking jewellery, watches, or the careless handling of money might sometimes be a temptation in what is a very poor country.

● Try not to linger, or look lost. The most dangerous areas are bus stations, markets, areas beyond the city centre, and isolated beaches, especially at night.

● In the unlikely event of a mugging, discretion is the better part of valour. Hand over your watch or money, try to stay calm, and you should be OK.

Left: *Flamboyant trees add a splash of colour to Dar es Salaam's otherwise uninspiring city centre.*

ASKARI MONUMENT

The Askari Monument pays tribute to the native troops who died in the 'Ice Cream War', the East African campaign during World War I, so-called because the British were convinced that their German enemies would 'melt away like ice cream in the sun'. The statue of the *askari* (which means soldier) seems to have surrendered to Dar's happy-go-lucky atmosphere, thrusting towards the harbour with a broken bayonet. The monument has come to symbolize the sacrifice made by all the native African troops, in conflicts which were not of Africa's making, but World War I alone caused the deaths, directly or indirectly, of 100,000 of them. The inscription on the monument was composed by Rudyard Kipling.

To get to know Dar it is best to walk, at least around the central areas. The main focal point, in the middle of Samora Machel Avenue, is the **Askari Monument**. Southwest of the monument **Samora Machel Avenue** stretches away in an untidy bustle of pedestrians and traffic. It is lined with dilapidated buildings, shops, restaurants and kiosks. Luxury goods to be found in the shops, such as electronic equipment and expensive household items, are imported, and visitors can usually buy the same things more cheaply back at home. Local products are often of poor quality, though hardwood furnishings and blackwood carvings often represent good value. But newcomers to Dar will be able to experience something of the city's easy-paced lifestyle, as well as something of its multi-cultural charm.

In the opposite direction Samora Machel, now lined with mature Pride of Bolivia trees, heads towards the open sea, by-passing the **old botanical gardens** on one side, and the **National Museum** on the other. The gardens are recently restored and are worth a visit. The National Museum contains, among other important relics, the skull

of 'Nutcracker Man' found by the Leakeys' at Olduvai – as well as some interesting displays of tribal artifacts and World War I memorabilia. The older part of the museum is a good example of British colonial architecture of the period. Just a little beyond the museum is **Karimjee Hall**, named after the Karimjee family, great benefactors to their adoptive country. The Hall is now used as Tanzania's Parliament Building.

Right: *One of Dar es Salaam's best-known landmarks, the Askari Monument.*

The seaward end of Samora Avenue terminates close to the **old German hospital**. It too is an interesting building, its lawns, baobabs and blossoming trees enlivening the stone solidity of the hospital itself. Its garden frontage offers a pleasant panorama of the sea and nearby shore.

Just to the south is the **State House**, with its own attractive lawns and trees. The official residence of the President, it is now partly screened by a wall and railings (photography is in any case forbidden in this area). The British rebuilt it in 1922 from the ruins of its German forerunner, which was shelled during World War I. The original building was sensitively re-designed, its white-painted front acknowledging Islamic influences.

Above: *The former chapel (and mortuary!) of the German Hospital, built in 1897 on Dar's Ocean Road.*

Kivukoni ★★

Beyond State House, where Ocean Road bends around towards Kivukoni Front, there is a fascinating little corner of Dar. Here the visitor can explore the **fish market**, watch the ships and small dhows coming and going through the narrow **harbour** entrance, and at the same time observe a captivating spectrum of Dar es Salaam's population going about its business.

Continuing past the fish market and the crowded corner by the ferry, the road, now Kivukoni Front, follows the curve of the harbour and offers fine views across the waterway on one side and the old German administration buildings, still in use, on the other. The road, lined by Indian almonds (*kungu*) on its seaward side, eventually passes the **Kilimanjaro Hotel**, the old **Dar es Salaam Club** and the **Lutheran Church**, with its cascade of red-tiled roofs, before merging with Sokoine

---

SHOPPING IN DAR

In terms of variety and quality, Arusha is a better place than Dar for handicrafts and souvenirs. But among the better products available in the capital are:
• Makonde carvings;
• hand-woven basketwork;
• batiks, and the *kitenge* that are worn by most Tanzanian women;
• Maasai beadwork;
• Zanzibar chests – although they are expensive and shipping home would have to be arranged – and other Zanzibar antiques, such as silver necklaces and broaches;
• African music cassettes, sold in most markets.

Right: *The rising edifice of St Joseph's Cathedral.*

Drive. Further along this road are the old German **Post Office**, **St Joseph's Cathedral**, the recently renovated **Boma** and the original **railway station**, built in Bavarian style.

Asian District *

The area enclosed in the irregular square formed by Samora Machel Avenue and UWT Street, and Uhuru and Maktaba, roughly corresponds to the town's Asian quarter. Here the visitor on foot can absorb a distinctly Indian flavour – both in atmosphere and more literally, for there are places selling spicy snacks such as samosas, *bhajias* (chilli bites), or those eastern mysteries known as *paan*, normally chewed as a digestive after meals. The Asian communities have brought their own colour to the expanding city. Most of them are traders, shopkeepers or business-people, and their peace-loving, family-based cultures, whether Hindu, Muslim or Sikh, continue to contribute to that most attractive of Dar es Salaam's charms, its friendly, easy-going cosmopolitanism.

Among these streets it always pays to look up, as well as around. The mosques (aligned towards Mecca), temples, little rooms above the shops, and the untidy clutter of crowded tenement blocks almost always have something to offer: an ornate balcony, intricately fretworked stone screens, an Islamic motif worked into the beauty of a mosque and a thousand and one little glimpses into the day-to-day life among the extended Asian families. Above many doorways you will see a string of dead leaves, put up to keep out evil spirits.

DAR'S BEACHES

• **Oyster Bay** beach is the closest to Dar, and is attractive and safe to swim from. It is particularly popular with local Asians, who gather there every evening at sunset in a cheerful social ritual. Visitors should be wary of petty thieves.
• Most of the main beach resorts are further north at **Kunduchi**. These include Bahari, Kunduchi, Rungwe Beach, Silver Sands, and Whitesands. These, with the exception of Bahari and Whitesands, are quite ordinary, but they all have swimming pools and a relaxing ambience. Some offer boat trips to nearby Bungoyo Island, where many people like to picnic. The Kunduchi beaches have suffered from erosion, and from the sometimes unlovely attempts to prevent it, but they are still pleasant.
• There is also a very good beach resort at **Ras Kutani**, an hour's drive south of Dar.

Kariakoo *

Another lively area – even more crowded, and inhabited mostly by Africans – lies to the northwest of UWT Street. It is called Kariakoo. At its centre is a large concrete **market hall**, but the nearby streets are a fascinating huddle of little *dukas* (shops), selling everything from plastic buckets to clothes, shoes and second-hand car spares.

Kariakoo gives visitors a brief insight into life among Dar es Salaam's more extensive and increasing African population. The majority live in simple Swahili-style huts or in flats in the less salubrious suburbs, but they maintain their own tribal customs and influences, their gregarious good nature and love of dancing, music and exuberant conversation.

Northern Suburbs **

Hassan Myinyi Street leads out of town to the north, and along it are three other noteworthy buildings: the *Nyumba ya Sanaa*, or **House of Art**, where visitors can buy a variety of African artifacts such as woven baskets, mats and batiks, the **Greek Orthodox Church** (in Romanesque Basilican style) and the **Ismaili Jama'at Khana**. The latter is a religious community centre for Ismaili Muslims, and during certain festivals, such as Idd or the Aga Khan's birthday, it is brilliantly illuminated. A little way to the north of Selander bridge by Haile Selassie Road stands **St Peter's Roman Catholic Church**, with its perforated screens and barrel-vaulted roof, and the **Little Theatre Club**, which normally has a lively repertoire, advertized in the local press.

OYSTER BAY'S WILD NIGHTLIFE

You might not see oysters in Oyster Bay, but occasionally you see less passive creatures. The suburbs are only 5km (3 miles) from Dar's crowded city centre, yet not too many years ago a lioness with cubs strolled optimistically through Oyster Bay and – to the relief of the inhabitants – out again. More recently a hippo climbed out of the sea (after being flushed from its normal home by floods) and grazed, every night, on the roadside verges. Visitors need have no qualms – they are unlikely to meet anything more dangerous than a minibus with bald tyres.

Below: Nyumba ya Sanaa, *the House of Art, near the Dar es Salaam Sheraton Hotel.*

Above: *Palm-fringed Oyster Bay, with the hotel of the same name alongside.*

Seaward are the leafy suburbs of **Oyster Bay**. The bay itself is quite pretty when seen from its southern cliffs in late afternoon, or when a full moon rises above the sea. Toure Drive, which follows the seafront, continues beyond the bay to Msasani peninsula, where the **Dar es Salaam Yacht Club** is situated.

The Bagamoyo Road carries on north from the city, passing the **Village Museum**, an authentic collection of traditional style huts, and the **University**, set on a low hill. The University has pleasant grounds, but the main tourist attraction in this area is **Mwenge Handicraft Market**, where the famous Makonde ebony carvers work and display their traditional sculptures. About 24km (15 miles) north of Dar es Salaam is **Kunduchi**, the main beach resort on this part of the coast, and the site of some interesting Arab ruins.

BAGAMOYO

The Bagamoyo Road deteriorates noticeably north of the Kunduchi turn-off, but passes through some attractive Swahili villages before reaching Bagamoyo itself. The small town, 70km (45 miles) from Dar, gives the impression of having slept through the 20th century. Its name is said to mean 'Here I lay down my heart', but whether this was a cry of despair from the countless slaves who were brought here, or a cry of relief from the returning caravan leaders and porters, is not certain.

History

As a terminal point on the coast for Arab trading caravans, Bagamoyo naturally became a holding depot for **slaves** brought from the interior. The fortified house, where slaves were kept before being led down a tunnel to

---

KUNDUCHI RUINS

Just inland from Kunduchi Village and adjacent to it are some early Arab tombs among the baobabs and coastal scrub. They are fine examples of their type, with unique pillars inscribed with Islamic chronologies and porcelain bowls set in the pillars. The delicate pottery bespeaks a fine life style among the coastal Arabs of the period, and with bowls from China and England, indicates the extent of the coast's worldwide trade links.

the sea and the dhows waiting to ship them across to Zanzibar, still stands, as does the tree under which many of them were sold locally. Not far from these reminders of misery is the *caravanserai* – a small inn – where the traders and porters celebrated their return and rested.

Men with other concerns passed through Bagamoyo. Among them were the brilliant **Burton** and the more taciturn **Speke**, who was soon, during his second expedition with Grant, to settle the age-old question of the Nile. In 1871 **H.M. Stanley**, with 192 men and six tonnes of equipment, strode off at his usual headlong pace to look for David Livingstone. He returned the following year in triumph, though at 31 his hair had turned grey and he was 'fearfully worn'.

Stanley last stayed in Bagamoyo for one eventful night in 1889, when his party (reduced to 196 from an original 708) marched into town after a three-year expedition across the continent. With him was **Emin Pasha**, governor of Equatoria, whom Stanley had rescued from the 'mad Mullah's' hordes. The Germans threw a lavish party at their headquarters (which still stands) to celebrate the return of the explorers. Emin, short-sighted and perhaps made unsteady by champagne, was later found unconscious, with blood dribbling from his ears. 'The Pasha', in the words of Evelyn Waugh, ' had taken a header off the balcony'.

LIVINGSTONE'S RETURN

David Livingstone died as he knelt in prayer in a village hut in what is now eastern Zambia. His faithful Zanzibari servants Abdulla Susi and James Chuma cut out his heart, buried it under a tree, and then took nine months to help carry his sun-dried remains, enwrapped in bark, to the coast. On arrival in Bagamoyo, the men laid down their burden outside the Mission Church, where they announced: 'Mwili wa Daudi' – 'The body of David'. The tale of that journey from the interior is one of the most moving stories in the annals of African exploration. By one of those ironies that seem inevitable in Africa, the body, in a new coffin of zinc and wood, was transported from Bagamoyo to Zanzibar on board *HMS Vulture*, before it was taken to London and buried in Westminster Abbey. The dour Scots missionary, not without humour, would have appreciated the joke.

Left: *The unpretentious streets of a once-important terminus of the slave and ivory trade, Bagamoyo.*

EMIN PASHA

Born Eduard Schnitzer to
Jewish parents in Prussian
Silesia, Emin joined the
Turkish army, and was
later appointed governor
of the Egyptian province of
Equatoria (roughly modern
Sudan). When the Arabs
turned on him, he was rescued by Stanley, and during
the celebrations for their safe
return to Bagamoyo in 1889
the Pasha, of poor sight and a
little tipsy, fell from a window
of the German headquarters.
He recovered from his frac-
tured skull but less than two
years later, sitting at a table in
his tent in the Congo peering
at his beloved specimens of
animals and plants, Arab slave
traders strolled in and un-
ceremoniously cut his throat.

Around Town

Bagamoyo itself is a motley collection of *dukas* (small shops) and huts, many of these in Swahili mud and wattle style, with thatched roofs. Some of the shops and houses have elaborately carved doors, though better examples are to be found in Zanzibar. It is easy to walk around Bagamoyo without too much exertion. Places worthy of note include the old **caravanserai,** the former **German headquarters** (there are two), and Bagamoyo's oldest building, a fortified **Arab house** begun in 1860 and later used as a prison (its 'hanging tree' still stands outside) and as a 'pen' for slaves awaiting shipment. A restoration programme is slowly preserving these and other historic buildings. Aside from history there is a pleasant **beach** as well as three simple but very relaxing beach hotels. The **Bagamoyo College of Arts**, just to the south of the town, is also worth visiting.

Mission **

Just outside the town to the north stands the first Catholic Mission in East Africa, built in 1868 by the Fathers of the Holy Ghost. Originally intended to house children rescued from slavery, it quickly expanded to become a church, a school, and a collection of workshops and farming projects. It was to this mission that Livingstone's body was brought in 1874.

Right: *The Fathers' House at Bagamoyo's historic Catholic Mission.*
Opposite: *Swahili ruins at Kaole, near Bagamoyo.*

The Mission remains much as it was then. The old buildings and a small, well-managed museum are the main attractions, but visitors might be interested to know that many exotic plants which now grace the streets and gardens of Tanzanian cities were first introduced here. Coffee was also planted.

The Kaole Ruins **

Five kilometres (3 miles) south of Bagamoyo are the Kaole ruins. They are basically medieval, though some structures (including the West Mosque, once perhaps the finest on the mainland) date back to the 3rd and 4th centuries. Kaole was once the main coastal trading centre between Kilwa and Mombasa, though like other towns of Zinj it declined with the coming of the Portuguese. Among its other notable buildings are a 15th-century house and some double 'love graves', which speak of the prosperous life (and death) styles that merchants enjoyed at the height of the Swahili civilization.

Saadani Game Reserve *

Saadani is Tanzania's only coastal wildlife sanctuary. It is relatively small (300km²; 116 sq miles) but it embraces a wide variety of habitats, which support an eclectic collection of animal and bird species, including at least 24 large mammal species (albeit in small numbers). In the dry season, away from the Wami River, water is scarce and animals less numerous, but the reserve is always worth visiting, except during heavy rains. Unless you can come to some arrangement with a travel company you will need to be completely self-sufficient. In Saadani Village, 50km (30 miles) north of Bagamoyo, there is an old German fort and some German graves.

THE BAGAMOYO CATHOLIC MISSION

In 1914 the peace of Bagamoyo was disturbed when the British mounted a naval bombardment and air attack on the town. As the Mission was left unmolested, the Germans moved most of their troops into its grounds, among the mango trees which still line the avenue from the Mission to the shore. Rather touchingly, they took three ancient, ornamental cannons from the Mission gardens and placed them among their more realistic defence battery. The British were neither fooled by the cannon nor deterred by the Mission's neutrality. They pounded the seafront and the mango trees, damaging the Fathers' House and the new church. Miraculously 2000 civilians sheltering in the Mission were unhurt. The German positions were soon overrun by a landing party and the garrison was taken.

Above: *Relics of once prosperous life styles, at Tongoni, by Tanga.*

BEES IN THEIR BONNETS

Sleepy little Tanga was the site of a fierce battle in 1914, when the British landed an 8000-strong assault force, mostly Indian troops, in an attempt to capture the Tanga railway line. Unfortunately the canny German commander, Von Lettow-Vorbeck, was given time to muster his forces. As the queasy assault force hit the beaches and struggled through the bush towards the town with bullets whipping around their turbans, they were attacked by a swarm of bees. It was more than enough for the attackers, who made a hasty retreat, leaving much of their equipment and morale behind. Some divisions took more casualties from the bees than the bullets, although the bullets proved more deadly, killing 800 and wounding 500.

TANGA AND PANGANI

Tanga is a small port some 230km (140 miles) up the coast from Dar. Its main street, along which troops of vervet monkeys sometimes roam, has an air of dilapidated colonial provincialism, but the town is a relaxing stopping-off point between Dar and Mombasa, and for dhows crossing from the harbour to Pemba Island.

Briefly the German capital, **Tanga** remains one of the larger towns in the country, relying mostly on exports of sisal. There are various places of interest, including the **Amboni Caves**, with limestone formations and colonies of fruit bats, the **Galanos Sulphur Springs** and the **Tongoni Ruins**, as well as some pleasant beaches. It is also possible to drive into the Usambara Mountains from the village of Muheza to **Amani**, an attractive little settlement surrounded by hills, forests and tea estates.

Pangani, on the estuary of the river of the same name and 45km (28 miles) south of Tanga, offers similarly quiet charms. It had fewer charms for the Arab rebel Abushiri, one of the leaders of an anti-German revolt, who was hanged by the Germans here in 1897, but present-day visitors might enjoy the waterfront and there are a few interesting buildings, including an Arab fort and some old slave-traders' mansions. The coastline in the area is very attractive and a luxury lodge, offering diving, snorkelling and big game fishing, is presently under construction, aiming to exploit the excellent off-shore opportunities.

SOUTH OF DAR

Immediately south of Dar es Salaam, across the Kivukoni ferry, are some beautiful beaches and a very pleasant beach resort, Ras Kutani. Beyond the beaches immediately south of Dar es Salaam, the coast is still largely undeveloped, its shoreline broken only by the watery maze where the Rufiji slides into the sea.

Kilwa *

One hundred kilometres (60 miles) south of the Rufiji Delta is the once-important settlement of Kilwa. Or rather the three Kilwas – Kilwa Kivinge and Kilwa Masoko, on their mainland peninsula, and the small island settlement of Kilwa Kisiwani. It is difficult now to believe that the Kilwas thrived on gold, slaves and ivory from the the 12th century, when it was first settled by Gulf Arabs, until the 1860s, when something like 20,000 slaves a year were shipped to servitude from its mangrove swamps. As early as 1502, when Vasco da Gama sailed in, an estimated 12,000 'black Moors' were living there.

Whatever spurious glamour **Kilwa Kivinge** once possessed, it has long since evaporated. **Kilwa Masoko** still flourishes, though the market from which it gets its name has nothing to do with slaves and everything to do with vegetables, fish and other local produce. But it is mostly the island of **Kilwa Kisiwani** which tourists and travellers seek out, for the ruins there represent the most exceptional examples of early Islamic architecture in sub-Saharan Africa.

The Far South

The rest of the Tanzanian coast, south of the Kilwas, awaits discovery and development. **Lindi** and **Mtwara**, in the far south, are drowsily awakening to the potentials of tourism, and for divers, snorkellers and anglers, or for those who enjoy the challenge of visiting relatively remote places, these towns by the ocean might be worth the trip. Visitors are, however, uncommon, and facilities for them are scarce.

THE KILWA RUINS

Some of the highlights of the outstanding ruins on Kisiwani Kilwa:

● The magnificent **Great Mosque**, beautiful even in decay. Built in the 12th century, it was entirely reconstructed in the 15th.

● Close by is the **Small Domed Mosque**. This, with its dome surmounted by a unique octagonal tower and its vaults once adorned by porcelain bowls, is perhaps the best-preserved of the island's ruins.

● One of the most impressive of the old buildings is **Husina Kubwa**, which commands a fine view across the straits from its vantage point on a projecting cliff. Husina means 'fort' in Arabic, but the building is thought to have been the palace of a wealthy ruler.

● There is a fort on the island, the **Geraza**, which dominates the northern shores. It was built by Omani Arabs in the early 19th century, on the foundations of a Portuguese stronghold.

Dar es Salaam and the Coast at a Glance

The months from **mid-May** to **mid-October** are relatively cool and not so humid, and rain is much less likely at this time of year. At other times the weather can be uncomfortably hot, especially from January to March, although monsoon breezes often alleviate the sultry heat. Rain in March and April, and to a lesser extent from mid-October to December, can be heavy and frustrating.

Dar es Salaam's international airport is served directly by **international flights**; however many people arrive here only to move on quickly towards the big game parks or Zanzibar.

Internal flights to Dar can be booked through Air Tanzania, tel: (051) 46643/ 44111. Charter companies, such as Coastal Travels, tel: (051) 37479/80/30934, fax: (051) 46045, and others are more expensive but much more reliable and straightforward.

Dar es Salaam and Tanga are accessible by good **roads** from Malawi, Zambia and Kenya in the north.

Luxury **buses** ply the Nairobi–Arusha–Dar routes; similar buses run from Moshi and Tanga to Dar. Most of them are recklessly driven and bus stations are often frequented by pick-pockets.

A reasonable but declining **railway** service links Dar with Zambia, and an older, less efficient service runs between Dar and Moshi and Tanga in the north.

Hydrofoils and other **ferries** connect Zanzibar with Dar several times daily. Offices and embarkation at Customs House jetty on seafront.

Buses are overcrowded and unreliable. A better option is a **taxi**. Official taxis have numbers painted on them in large black letters and taxi indicators on their roof; there are pirate taxis operating, but these are best avoided. The best option for visitors is to use the services of a **tour company**. Among the best of the tour companies are: Coastal Travels, Savannah Tours, Selous Safari Co. Good value for money can often be found with less prominent firms such as Takim's or Walji's.

Car-hire firms include: Avis, Ghana Ave, tel: (051) 30505/34562/34598, fax: (051) 37426/37442.
Europcar, tel: (051) 862975, fax: (051) 862973.
Hertz, Sheraton Hotel foyer, tel: (051) 25237/25753.
These firms also have desks at Dar airport.

Dar es Salaam
Sheraton, tel: (051) 32546, fax: (051) 30145. Newly

opened, the first five-star hotel in Dar. Situated on the edge of town, with 240 standard rooms plus executive suites.
New Africa, tel: (051) 29611, fax: (051) 29610. Centrally situated close to the harbour, with 240 rooms including seven suites, swimming pool, casino and roof-top restaurant
Kilimanjaro, tel: (051) 21281/ 46520, fax: (051) 46762. Long-established and central, with 198 rooms. Once Dar's premier hotel and now being upgraded. Includes swimming pool, nightclub, roof-top restaurant offering fine view over the harbour.
Oyster Bay, tel: (051) 68631, fax: (051) 68631. Pleasantly situated by a reasonable beach a little way outside town. Has 20 rooms, an open-fronted restaurant overlooking the sea and a beer garden.

BEACH HOTELS CLOSE TO DAR
Whitesands, tel: (051) 44484/ 35801, fax: (051) 39885/ 44476. Located north of Dar, with 44 air-conditioned rooms in thatched chalets. Expensive by Dar standards, but offers casino, disco, five bars, a restaurant serving Continental, Chinese, Indian and Tanzanian specialities, swimming pool and coffee shop. Claims four-star status.
Bahari, tel: (051) 47101/2. Attractively designed, with 100 air-conditioned rooms, open-sided restaurant facing the sea and a swimming pool.

Dar es Salaam and the Coast at a Glance

Ras Kutani, contact Coastal Travels or Selous Safari Co. The best mainland beach resort close to Dar, an hour-and-a-half's drive south across the Kigamboni ferry. Secluded, well-situated and designed, with 25 self-contained cottages built around a fresh-water lagoon. Good food, watersports.

Bagamoyo
Bagamoyo Beach Resort, tel: 900 and ask for Bagamoyo 83. Simple, clean, good French cooking.
Traveller's Lodge. Simple and clean with reasonable food.

Tanga and Pangani
Kingfisher Lodge, tel: (053) 42491. A former private house converted into a four-bedroomed lodge situated by the sea at Kigamboni.
Mashado Game Fishing Lodge. Due to open in early 1996. Luxury five-star cliff-top lodge with air-conditioned cottages. Excellent game fishing in Pemba Channel and good diving and snorkelling.

Mtwara
M'Simbati Estate. Also due to open in 1996. Boasts remote beaches, fine diving, snorkelling, windsurfing, sailing, fishing, bird watching and village visits.
Ruvala Camp. Low-impact luxury camp, offering similar facilities to M'Simbati Estate. Information on both resorts

is available only through International Ventures, Wilton, Connecticut, USA, tel: (203) 761-1110, fax: (203) 762-7104.

WHERE TO EAT

Most restaurants in Dar are quite ordinary when compared with those in other parts of the world, but numbers and standards are rising. The better ones include:
Sheraton: Best in town.
Alcove: Good Indian food, but can be too oily for western tastes. Centrally situated.
Casanova: Italian. Good and pleasantly situated in shopping mall out of town.
Dolce Vita: Italian. Interesting thatched structure by the sea.
Night of Istanbul: Basically Turkish. Meals are filling and reasonable. Centrally situated.
Rickshaw: In a converted private house in outer suburbs. Best Chinese food in town.
Smokies Tavern: Also in the outer suburbs, but more pleasantly situated by the sea. Good value British-style cuisine, especially for those who love seafood. Very popular. The restaurants at the **Oyster Bay Hotel** and the **Kilimanjaro Hotel's Summit Restaurant** are worth trying.

TOURS AND EXCURSIONS

Tours of Dar: A few companies arrange tours around the main sights of the city and surrounds. Otherwise the best way to get around the city centre is to walk.
Excursions to Zanzibar: Day trips are quite feasible on the regular ferry and hydrofoil services; check seafront offices for times. Boats (including dhows) can be chartered through Coastal Travels to take you to various coastal destinations, including Ras Kutani and Kilwa.
Day trips to Bagamoyo: The history makes it worthwhile although the 75 km (45 mile) road isn't good.

USEFUL CONTACTS

Code for Dar: 051.
Emergencies: 999.
Operator: 900.
Coastal Travels: tel: (051) 37479, fax: (051) 46045.
Savannah Tours: tel: (051) 25752, fax: (051) 44568.
Selous Safari Co: tel: (051) 34802, fax: (051) 46980.
Air Tanzania: tel: (051) 46643/44111.
Dar es Salaam International Airport: tel: (051) 42111.
Precision Air: tel: (051) 30800.

DAR ES SALAAM	J	F	M	A	M	J	J	A	S	O	N	D
AVERAGE TEMP. °F	81	81	81	79	75	75	75	75	75	77	79	81
AVERAGE TEMP. °C	27	27	27	26	26	26	26	26	26	25	26	27
HOURS OF SUN DAILY	8	9	7	5	6	8	8	8	8	8	9	9
RAINFALL ins.	2	3	4	11	9	1	1	1	1	2	3	3
RAINFALL mm	49	75	114	289	216	25	27	24	37	63	73	83
DAYS OF RAINFALL	3	5	9	18	13	4	4	5	6	6	6	9

3
The Land of Kilimanjaro

As wide as all the world, great, high and unbeliev-ably white in the sun. . . .' For a writer who made the adjective an endangered species, four in one sentence is a rare extravagance. Hemingway, we can suppose, was impressed by Kilimanjaro.

With good reason, for the mountain he describes is remarkably beautiful. And the land over which it rises, in such imposing isolation, is scarcely less so. To the west, beyond farms and fields of coffee, the dark pyramid of **Mount Meru** towers above **Arusha National Park**. Beyond Meru a volcanic landscape sweeps up to the Kenyan border and down towards the **Rift Valley**.

South of the two great mountains stretches the so-called Maasai Steppe, with **Tarangire National Park** in its northwest corner, while southeast of Kilimanjaro the **Pare Mountains** diminish towards the coast in a pleasing swirl of hills, valleys, and eventually savanna, much of it enclosed in one of Tanzania's loveliest game sanctuaries, **Mkomazi**. The Pare ranges are continued south by the **Usambaras**, rich in endemics and scenic splendour.

The two towns found in the region are small, but both are of significance to most visitors. **Moshi**, the quiet, strangely pious centre of the Chagga homelands, stands closest to Kilimanjaro on the mountain's lower southern slopes. Its more secular counterpart and tourist capital of the region, **Arusha**, lies below Meru. Little more than a crossroads on the highway to the famous northern game parks beyond the Rift, Arusha exudes a frontier-town

CLIMATE

The dry months from June to October are cool, especially in the evenings and early mornings, when the mean temperature drops to 15°C (59°F). Daytime temperatures, even in the dry season, can be quite hot on the plains, but humidity is low compared with the coast. The wettest months are March and April, when some park tracks can be impassable, with a shorter rainy season mid-October to mid-December.

Opposite: *Mt Kilimanjaro rising out of the clouds; a Masaai herdboy looks on from the Kenyan side.*

DON'T MISS

*** Kilimanjaro: to climb, to see, or just to be near.
** Arusha National Park: splendid scenery, and walks to Mt Meru.
** Tarangire National Park: loved by connoisseurs; at its finest in the dry season, large concentrations of game.
* Mkomazi Game Reserve: lovely wild scenery, though game is relatively scarce.
* Lushoto: fewer tourists, but magnificent mountain and forest scenery.

functionality, its unpretentious shops as likely to sell clutch plates as curios. But it retains a lingering prettiness which, when its jacarandas are purple-blue with blossoms, aspires to beauty.

KILIMANJARO ***
History and Background

Many tourists arrive in the north of Tanzania at Kilimanjaro airport. If they land by daylight they will usually be treated to a spectacular view of a most spectacular mountain, which dominates, physically and figuratively, the entire plains from which it rises. Thought to be dormant rather than dead, Kilimanjaro is young in geological terms, having been created during massive eruptions about 750,000 years ago. Despite the fact that the area of its base is larger than that of Greater London, and that it is said to be the highest free-standing mountain in the world, Kilimanjaro remained unknown to the west until 11 May 1848. On that day the German missionary **Johannes Rebmann**, armed with his Bible and umbrella, fancied he saw, on the summit of one of the 'mountains of Jagga' (as he called the three clouded peaks of Kilimanjaro), a 'dazzling white cloud'. His guide laconically told him that the cloud was *baridi* – cold. Rebmann realized that what he was looking at was snow.

Opposite: *Kilimanjaro National Park headquarters, the starting point for ascents up the mountain by the Marangu route.*

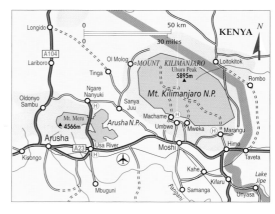

His reports were ridiculed by distinguished geographers. The idea of a snow-topped mountain just south of the equator seemed absurd, but the gentle missionary was of course right. It was over 40 years before another German, **Dr Hans Meyer**, and an alpine guide, **Ludwig Purtscheller**, became the first men to climb the loftiest of the great mountain's three peaks, Kibo, at 5896m (19,340ft) the highest point in Africa

The **Chagga** who live on its slopes have no word for the whole mountain which is at the centre of their lives, only for its two main peaks, Kibo and Mawenzi. No-one really knows how Kilimanjaro got its popular name, but ironically the word *Kilima* in Kiswahili means hill rather than mountain. Perhaps the diminutive was used out of familiarity, for Kilimanjaro (or 'Kili', to many) seems to inspire affection among all those who have come to know her. The famous 'Christmas pudding' mountain is instantly familiar all over the world, often from photographs taken from Amboseli National Park in Kenya. Its popularity is enhanced by the fact that many thousands of visitors reach the summit each year, and Kili can justifiably claim to be the highest mountain in the world accessible to non-expert mountaineers.

THE CHAGGA

To the Chagga the importance of Kilimanjaro cannot be over-emphasized. The mountain gives them shelter and its slopes sustenance, but above all it gives them an identity: an old, precise, deep-rooted sense of place. A Bantu-speaking race, visitors will meet them as guides and porters on Kili, and they are considered one of the most enterprising, forward-looking people in Tanzania. One feature of their culture is that their language is rich in place-names. The most ordinary stream will have a name of its own, helping to place it in the mental maps and the 'tribal memory' of the local people, and incidentally reflecting the importance of water to a people who can see, from their mountain home, the dust-storms blowing across the baked red earth of the plains below.

Moshi *

Moshi stands on the lower southern slopes of Kilimanjaro, but it is often bypassed on the way to the start of the climb at Marangu. It has the most magnificent setting, but as a town it is respectable rather than exciting. The international airport is 34km (21 miles) to the west, and the town is also accessible by rail and road. Arusha, an hour's drive to the west of Moshi, is the nearest sizeable centre, while a further three hours drive to the north and into Kenya is Nairobi, a well-established tourist centre.

GETTING HIGH ON KILI

Some of the most commonly
related of Kilimanjaro's tales
are those of altitude sickness.
Even the fittest athlete can
succumb to this humiliating
and unpleasant illness, and
popular though climbing
Kili is, it is not something
to be undertaken lightly.
• The effects of altitude
sickness start around 3500m
(10,500ft). The symptoms
are a loss of appetite,
sleeplessness, headaches,
nausea and fatigue.
• The best ways to deal with
it are to take plenty of liquid,
carbohydrate and sleep when
you can, to climb *pole pole*
(slowly), and to spend a
second night at Horombo
hut acclimatizing. If things
get really bad, descend.
It's an instant cure.
• Other dangers on the
mountain are the severe
cold on the summit, which
demands proper equipment
(it can be hired from
Marangu), and the sun,
which many forget about.
• There is a mountain rescue
team on the mountain.
Everyone climbing the
mountains pays a rescue
fee to cover this service.

The village of **Marangu**, less than an hour's drive east of Moshi, is the starting point for most ascents of the mountain. A number of operators are based here, as well as the area's two famous hotels, the Kibo and the Marangu. It is a pleasant village with an alpine feel, and lies 7km (4 miles) from the entrance to the National Park gate, which marks the start of the Marangu, or tourist, route up Kilimanjaro.

Climbing Kilimanjaro **

From Marangu, at 1500m (5000ft), the mountain can look very imposing, but would-be climbers have little to fear except over-booking on the popular tourist route, and the pretty awful effects of altitude sickness. Tens of thousands of people climb Kili every year, and tens of thousands come safely down again. Most people opt for the standard five-day climb, though some people choose to spend an extra night at the second of the trail's three huts, to help acclimatize.

Day One: The first stage of the climb is through the rain forest, a lovely three- or four-hour trek from the park entrance to the first complex of A-frame huts, named after the famous Chagga chief **Mandara**, at 2700m (8850ft). The forest zone, which girdles the mountain, is

Right: *In the dank, sultry air of the rainforest at the start of the climb, the snow and ice of the summit seems a long way away.*

Left: *Day one of the climb, through the forest zone.*

the second of the five distinctive vegetative zones walkers experience on their ascent. It has a characteristic rain-forest atmosphere; a damp, green luxuriance which for some people is claustrophobic. Among the mighty trees, festooned with vines and lichens, Sykes or Colobus monkeys are sometimes seen, as is the brilliant crimson flash of a Hartlaub's turaco. As the path approaches Mandara Hut one encounters the first groves of giant heather.

Day Two: After an overnight stop at Mandara, walkers press on (or more wisely saunter) to the second complex of huts at **Horombo**, at 3720m (12,200ft). Skirting Maundi Crater to the west, the track climbs a fairly steep and sometimes slippery bank of rainforest, soon emerging on to the heathland zone, which in turn becomes upland moors. This is beguiling country of open views and muted moorland colours, where modest but beautiful plants abound. The plants are tougher than they look, and it is easy for the walker to forget that this gentle, rolling country is higher than the peaks of the Pyrenees. *Pole pole* is the order of the day, for the last few kilometres of the five-hour walk to Horombo involves some small but deceptively tiring ravines.

BIBULOUS BARONS AND CAROUSING COUNTS

Climbing Kilimanjaro can seem a bit of a dawdle these days, but getting there first was a bit more daunting.
● In 1861 the German explorer **Von der Decken** attempted Kilimanjaro but saw off his celebratory magnum of champagne (and his chances of reaching the summit) long before he emerged from the foothills.
● 16 years later Hungarian bon viveur **Count Samuel Teleki** and his companion paid similar respects to a bottle of red wine as they camped in the snow on The Saddle. They got little further.
● In 1889, **Hans Meyer** and **Ludwig Purtscheller** reached the crater rim after an exhausting climb over the crevasse-ridden ice-cap. Weakened and wearied they staggered back to camp, but the next morning (3 October) they returned, eventually reaching the highest point in Africa. Meyer planted a small German flag, the two men shook hands, raised three cheers for their Kaiser, and called the peak Kaiser Wilhelm Spitze – now Uhuru (Freedom) Point.

PICTURE PERFECT

Kilimanjaro, like the zebra, is irresistible to photographers. The mountain hasn't been known to move in the last 75,000 years, but your hands often do (camera shake is the most common reason for poor amateur photos). The pros recommend:

● Using a **tripod** and shutter release cable.

● Using a **slow film** (eg ASA 64), and as small an aperture as conditions allow.

● Preparing your equipment beforehand, and getting up early to get the best **light**.

● Finding an interesting **viewpoint**. The garden of the Marangu Hotel, the vista across the lakes in Arusha National Park, and the airplane window (flights usually pass to the east, so book a seat on the appropriate side!) are some suggestions.

● At the **summit**, you won't be in the best of moods to take masterpieces, but try and get a few snaps as you're unlikely to be back. The extreme cold might affect your camera mechanisms, and batteries run down much quicker. Pop them in your pocket to keep them warm.

Day Three: Just after Horombo climbers pass a stream known ominously as Last Water then some low, striated cliffs known as Zebra Rocks. Ahead is the Saddle, the sway-backed ridge which connects Kilimanjaro's two main peaks, **Kibo** and **Mawenzi**. Beyond Zebra Rocks the track forks. The path to the right is the more direct route to the Saddle, the gradual path to the left the more frequently recommended route. Whatever route is taken, the Saddle is not a welcoming place. The five- or six-hour walk is quite gentle, but the last upcurve to **Kibo Hut**, at 4700m (15,400ft), can turn legs to sandbags and make hearts go into overdrive.

Days Four and Five: Kibo Hut is a dreary place at the best of times, with an atmosphere as congenial as a condemned cell in Siberia. Walkers huddle into sleeping bags, not to sleep but to keep warm. Heads pounding, stomachs churning, they wait to be dragged out, at 01:00 or 02:00, into the icy darkness. Then, with a guide leading the way holding a small lantern, each party files into the night up the steep, zigzag track which leads to **Gillman's Point** on the summit crater rim. The early start allows walkers to reach Gillman's by dawn and to see the spectacular sunrise beyond Mawenzi and, with the scree freezing at night, provides a safer footing. But the third

Right: *Kibo peak looms large for climbers on the Mweka route.*

reason for making this final ascent in darkness is to maintain a visual ignorance; if walkers could see what lies ahead, how steep the slope is, how high above them the rocks were that mark the last scramble to the rim, they might well lose heart and turn back.

And so they plod on, mountain sticks tapping out a slow, staccato rhythm. The guide sometimes sings a plaintive song, to placate the mountain, and to take the minds of his charges off their ordeal. At this altitude, oxygen is twice as rare as it would be at sea level; breathing becomes laborious, paced steps and frequent stops are important. Almost every step becomes an effort of will. Halfway to Gillman's Point (and about two hours above Kibo Hut) is an overhang known as Hans Meyer cave, in which walkers often take a breather.

Above the cave the track rises very steeply. Walkers are faced with a further two hours of will and energy-sapping endeavour. At Johannes Notch, on the crater rim, there is a last heavy-legged scramble to Gillman's, and relative relief. Few people leap around in triumph, and the view which is revealed to them, as the sun climbs up beyond the turreted peaks of Mawenzi, far across The Saddle, does not always manage to gladden the thumping heart. Most people yearn only for those three much-recommended cures for altitude sickness – descent, descent, descent.

Above: *Evening light on the exposed Barafu spur, one of the setting-off points for the final early-morning push to the summit.*

STRANGE THINGS AT THE TOP OF AFRICA

Animals, as well as flowers, have been seen at the top of Kilimanjaro, including the frozen carcass of a leopard, mentioned by Hemingway in *The Snows of Kilimanjaro*, and a small pack of wild dogs reported by that great explorer, Wilfred Thesiger. Odd things have gone on there too. Parachutists have landed on Kibo, hang-gliders have jumped off it, it has been climbed by a pair with their legs tied together, a party of blind people, an 85-year old Spaniard (who vows he'll be back when he's 90), a motor-cyclist has conquered it and a game of tiddlywinks has been played at the summit.

ARRANGEMENTS FOR CLIMBING KILIMANJARO

• With all park fees payable in foreign currency, climbing Kilimanjaro is expensive, and becoming more so. You are required to hire a registered **guide**, and of course porters will make the ascent a lot less burdensome.

• Most tourists arrange their climb through an operator in Arusha, Moshi, or Marangu, who offer **package deals**. Make sure these include park and hut fees, the rescue fee, guides and porters, food, and transport to and from the park gate. An all-in package for a five-day climb will cost from around US$600 upwards with US$120–150 for each extra day. Cheaper deals are available, but are often less reliable.

• Make sure you have warm and wind-proof **clothing**, appropriate and comfortable footwear, a decent sleeping bag, sun protection and water bottles. Equipment can be hired at Marangu, but again you have to be wary of quality, which becomes important on the crucial final stages of your climb.

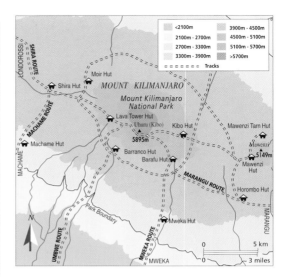

That view, which means so little to so many at the time, will later live with them forever. And the punishment and pain will all be forgotten. For to look down on Africa, from the top of Africa's highest mountain, is truly breathtaking. And the peak itself, with its wedding cake-like terraces of ice, and perhaps a fresh layer of snow in and around the symmetry of its remarkable crater, has a stark and sterile beauty of its own.

The true summit, **Uhuru Point**, is 210m (700ft) higher,

and a further hour's struggle around the crater rim. For many Gillman's is enough, and almost everyone is glad when the time comes to go down. The descent down the loosening scree should be treated with caution, but the long trek back from the base of Kibo to Mandara Hut is covered, by most people, surprisingly quickly (Horomobo Hut being bypassed).

Left: *A high campsite on the Shira plateau.*
Opposite: *On the roof of Africa. Smile and pretend you don't have a headache!*

Other Routes

There are other trails on the mountain besides the Marangu (or Tourist Route), which some consider to be overcrowded. These are more private and perhaps more attractive, though overnight accommodation is basic and camping might be necessary on some routes. Of these trails, the **Machame** is regarded as the most beautiful, a lovely gradual ascent through the forest bringing walkers out on to the moorland of the Shira plateau, facing the magnificent Western Breach with its daunting Wall (rated by Reinhold Messner, one of the greatest mountaineers of all time, as 'more serious than the North Face of the Eiger'). The Machame, **Umbwe** and **Mweka** routes all ascend the south-facing slopes of Kili, while the **Shira** route approaches from the west but is harder to get to.

Vegetation

One of the many interesting effects of a five-kilometre-high free-standing mountain on the Equator is that it embraces a complete range of vegetational zones. On the lowest slopes, up to a height of about 1800m (5900ft), the land, of rich volcanic soil, is used for **pasture** and **cultivation**. The next zone is composed of **rainforest**. With an annual rainfall of over 2000mm (79in), it is lush, dense, and often girdled by mist. The rain and condensation filters through the plants,

KILI BITES

Those without the time or inclination to climb to the summit of Kilimanjaro might want to enjoy the mountain in a few different ways:
● A pleasant day trip is to walk as far as the **first hut** (3 hours), and Maundi Crater just beyond, which has some fine views across the Kenyan border.
● You can drive over into **Kenya** at Taveta, and one and a half hours further is Lake Jipe. From Lake Jipe Lodge there are famous views back to Kilimanjaro, often enhanced by a couple of elephants wandering across the foreground.
● The little town of **Marangu** itself is a pretty place and rich in Chagga history, like all the old Chagga chiefdoms. There are pleasant walks, including a short trek to a lovely waterfall. And at least one traditional bee-hive hut remains, with its underground tunnels and bolt-holes, used, in the old days, during attacks by other clans, or by the Maasai from the plains.

A FEW COMMON BIRDS OF THE MOORLAND

Kilimanjaro's famous giant lobelia hides some pretty flowers, which are visited by scarlet-tufted malachite sunbirds. The male is a metallic green bird with a long tail, its tiny scarlet tufts sometimes visible on either side of its chest. The smaller Eastern double-collared sunbird is also found here. Other, less colourful birds to be seen on the moorland include augur and mountain buzzards, Shelley's francolins, Cape quail, Alpine swifts, stone chats, Hunter's cisticolas and yellow-crowned canaries. Alpine chats, streaky seed-eaters and white-necked ravens might be seen around Horombo Hut. The chats are as tame and as perkily plump as European redbreasts. They might well be called the 'Kilimanjaro Robin' but they are true mountain birds, at home on the upland moors.

humus, and porous volcanic rock. The water then runs underground along less porous strata of lava to emerge as springs on the lower slopes, where much of it is channelled into the sometimes ancient and ingenious irrigation schemes of the Chagga. Most of the wildlife found on the mountain occurs in the forest, including elephant, buffalo and leopard, but walkers are very unlikely to encounter them. More common are black and white colobus monkey, or the blue-grey Sykes monkey, along with a number of birds.

From about 2800m (9200ft) to 4000m (13,100ft), the landscape becomes open **heath** and **moorland**. This is characterized by hardy heathers, some of which grow up to 9m (30ft) tall, and giant lobelias and senecios. *Lobelia deckenii*, the only giant lobelia found on Kilimanjaro, can sometimes grow up to 3m (10ft) in height. *Senecio kilimanjari* is one of two giant senecios found on the moors. It too is endemic, and grows as high as 5m (16ft). The senecios have thick shaggy stems, often branched, and are topped by great rosettes of leaves, like giant artichokes with open bracts. Like the lobelias they grow beside streams. Behind Horombo Huts, in the damp little valley below Mawenzi, a whole colony of them stand like monsters from another world.

Right: *A rare, giant* senecio kilimanjari *on the moorland zone.*

Above this, from 4000m (13,100ft), is the **'Alpine'** **desert**. It seems very bleak, ranging from freezing temperatures at night to blistering sunlight at midday. This constant freezing and thawing (called solifluction), loosens the soil, discouraging the growth of roots, but lichens are common, while one plant, a moss ball, rolls around feeding on the soil it picks up and the moisture it absorbs.

Little lives above 5000m (16,400ft), and though the **glaciers** of the summit are slowly reducing in size, much of the ground is constantly under ice and snow. One everlasting flower, *Helichrysum newii*, has learned to live in Kibo Crater, sustained by the heated soil alongside a fumarole. It is said to be the highest flower on earth.

ARUSHA

Arusha, 70km (45 miles) to the west of Moshi, is a livelier town than its neighbour. Situated beneath Mount Meru, it is base camp for most safaris in Tanzania's famous northern game reserves. Like many African towns, it has a half-neglected air, but tourism is bringing in money, hope and rising standards. A decent range of hotels, restaurants and curio shops are now springing up, and Arusha could well develop into the Nairobi of northern Tanzania.

CLIMBING MOUNT MERU

Guided climbs to the 4566m (14,990ft) high summit of Meru can be arranged. The ascent can be done in two days, but three is advisable. It is a pleasant climb, without the crowds or severe altitude problems associated with Kilimanjaro, and big game is more common in the forest zone. Costs are lower as well, although you will need a registered guide, and good equipment is necessary to combat the cold on the upper slopes. The most common itinerary is to walk from Momela Gate to Miriakamba Hut on the first day, which allows a chance to explore the fantastic crater and ash cone. Day two is only a three hour climb to Saddle Hut, at 3600m (11,800ft), from where the summit (4566m; 14,950ft) is four to five hours away, and normally attempted early the next morning. Coming down to Momela Gate takes about eight to nine hours. The best time to climb Meru is between October and February.

Left: *Arusha, the unassuming hub of Tanzania's beautiful and fascinating northern safari circuit.*

Above: *Ships in the desert sailing unfamiliar waters in the lee of Mount Meru.*

NGURDOTO CRATER

One of Arusha Park's prime attractions is Ngurdoto Crater. No human incursions on to the crater floor are permitted, and visitors must drive to the crater rim to look down into its entrancing green arena. It is 3km (2 miles) in diameter, and its forests and swamps are home to elephant, buffalo and other creatures. Red duiker might be observed in the forest during the steep ascent, and colobus monkeys, those handsome acrobats of the high canopy, are often to be seen close to one of the viewpoints on the crater rim.

Mount Meru ★★

Like its more renowned cousin to the East, Mount Meru is volcanic, but its dark peaks and ridges are more mountain-like than the Christmas pudding Kilimanjaro, its collapsed crater floor being tucked away amid the forest, far below the summit. This crater is a most impressive place, silent, almost eerie, half-encircled by a ghostly forest of lichen-hung trees. A precipitous ash cone rises from it, backed by its own darkly forbidding wall, over 1500m (4900ft) high. Meru is part of Arusha National Park, and it is possible to walk to the crater through the rainforest, from the park's Momela Gate. The ascent is straightforward and takes about three or four hours.

There are elephant and buffalo on Meru, and the possibility of strolling around a corner to find several tonnes of muscle and bone twitching, stamping and snorting demands that you are accompanied by an armed ranger. The actual danger is minimal, but there might be times when this is hard to believe. Less threatening creatures live here too, among them the shy and handsome bushbuck. Sensitive walkers, if they stay silent and still, might get good views of these.

Arusha National Park ★★

The park which Meru overlooks is overlooked in a
different sense by many tourists, who rush by to more
spectacular places, yet Arusha National Park is among
the most beautiful in Africa. With Meru in its western
corridor, and Kilimanjaro over to the east, it encompasses
placid alkaline lakes, montane forest and open glades. Its
rhino have been obliterated and its elephant, harassed
by poachers, have largely taken to the hills, but Arusha
retains a superb range of flora and fauna. Other mammals
in the park include leopard, hyena, baboon, hippo, zebra,
giraffe, waterbuck, dik-dik and warthog. Bird life is
prolific, especially around the **Momella Lakes**, which
often host flamingoes, pelicans, herons and waders.

THE FRINGES OF THE MAASAI STEPPE
Tarangire National Park ★★

A very different, but perhaps even more exciting
National Park, is Tarangire, across the Ardai Plains west
of Arusha. Named after the shallow but important river
which passes through it, Tarangire is 'on' when the
southern Serengeti is 'off', with huge numbers of game
sustained by the river through the dry season.

The Park is one of the few places in Africa where
elephants can sometimes be seen in herds of 300 or more,
and lion are quite common,
especially during the dry season when the huge numbers of
wildebeest and zebra trek in
from the Steppe tired and
unwary. Black rhino were once
common, but were almost all
exterminated in the 1980s.
There is also an impressive
number and diversity of birds,
while the very country itself,
particularly in the north areas
with their umbrella thorns and
elephant-battered boababs,
is quintessential 'real Africa'.

Below: *The Tarangire
River provides welcome
relief in an otherwise dessicated dry-season landscape.*

Right: *Elephants, living barometers of successful management in many game parks, on the move in Mkomazi.*

FLIES, DAMN FLIES, AND STATISTICS

Tsetse flies, which are rather like greyish house-flies with wings which overlap when folded, can cause sleeping sickness in domestic stock and humans, but cases involving tourists are almost unknown, and the disease can be successfully treated. Like the mosquito, it feeds on blood, but unlike the mosquito, the tsetse's proboscis is relatively thick and saw-toothed, and the bites are like a jab with a big needle. The good news is that the flies keep the Maasai and similar cattle-herders out of Tarangire and other parks, without harming the game, which is why so many sanctuaries were set aside in the first place. It is estimated that a wart-hog (the tsetse's favourite host) 'donates' an estimated 20g (0.7oz) of blood a day.

Mkomazi *

Across the Maasai Steppe, 125km (78 miles) or so south of Moshi, is another game sanctuary, Mkomazi. Access is via **Same** township through a gap in the Pare Mountains.

From these lovely ranges German guns once bombarded the British-led forces as they chased their elusive enemies south during World War I. Same is peaceful now, and the Pare people are gentle and obliging, though hunters with bows and arrows can still be seen close to the town. But those one-time warriors, the Maasai, have recently been evicted from the reserve and are fighting (in the courts, not with spears) for what they see as their traditional grazing rights. Any resolution which gives Mkomazi's animals full protection without denying limited grazing to the Maasai would surely benefit Tanzania's tourist industry. The Maasai are always a cultural attraction, and Mkomazi is a beautiful place, especially after the rains, when its sweeping hills and plains are a vibrant green.

Mkomazi's game is still quite wild despite decades of poaching and hunting, and although visitors might not see as much, in terms of numbers, as they will in the better-known sanctuaries, the reserve is as pretty a piece of bush as you are likely to see in Africa and any animals are a bonus. Among those present are lion, leopard, cheetah, elephant, buffalo, eland, fringe-eared oryx, hartebeest, zebra, giraffe, Grant's gazelle and the shy aardwolf. Birding is excellent.

Lushoto *

South of Same and the Pares are the **Western Usambaras**, another lovely range of mountains. A pleasant 110km (70 miles) drive from Mkomazi, with the mountains to the east and the Maasai plains to the west, brings the traveller to **Mombo**. From here a good road winds up into the Usambaras to Lushoto, 25km (15 miles) away. The drive alone is worth the diversion, for the scenery, especially in good light, is extremely picturesque.

Lushoto, sited on the slopes and terraces of a pleasant upland valley, was obviously popular with the colonial Germans, who, acknowledging its situation and relatively mild climate, thought at one time of making it their capital. Even now the administrative buildings, missions and churches around the town proclaim their European derivation. The vicinity of Lushoto is very fertile, producing vegetables and fruits for the markets of Dar and elsewhere.

> **WALKING IN THE UMBASARAS**
>
> There are some fine walking tracks around Lushoto, many of them gently graded paths leading through the montane forest or up the hillsides. Although widely cultivated, the western Umbasaras offer some magnificent scenery, and the forests protect a spectacular number of endemic plants. One of the most rewarding walks is to a place called The Viewpoint, a comfortable one-hour hike from Lushoto, via Irente. The views from this vantage point, across the course of the Pangani and the Maasai Steppe beyond, are very impressive. Ask at the hotels for other recommendations.

Below: *The expanse of the Maasai plains and the small town of Mombo.*

The Land of Kilimanjaro at a Glance

The northern areas are generally pleasant throughout the year, except for the rainy periods from mid-March to mid-May and mid-October to mid-December. The months from **mid-May** to **mid-October** are normally dry and cooler. The driest months for climbing Kilimanjaro are **July** to **September**, and to a lesser extent January and February.

Most tourists to Tanzania travel on a pre-arranged Kenya/Tanzania **package tour**. Alternatives include: Kilimanjaro Airport is served by direct **flights** from countries within and outside Africa; internal flights are available through Air Tanzania; flight time between Dar and Kilimanjaro is about 40 minutes. Air charter companies also operate.
Most of the northern region east of the Rift is now served by good **roads** and by long-distance **buses**. Journeys between Dar and Moshi take 7–8 hours, Dar and Arusha 8–9 hours, and Dar and Nairobi 11–12 hours. Many tourists travel from Nairobi to Arusha via Namonga. The road is quite good and the drive takes about 3–4 hours. Moshi has a **rail** link with Dar es Salaam and Tanga, but the overnight trip takes about 16 uncomfortable hours.

The best way to get around northern Tanzania is with a dependable **tour company**. There are 120 such companies in Arusha alone, and a few in Moshi. Among the better ones are Abercrombie and Kent, Ker and Downey, Pollman's, UTC and Wilderrun. Other recommended companies in Arusha include Hoopoe Adventure Tours, Leopard Tours, Savannah Tours and Scan-Tan. In Moshi, Trans-Kibo Travels and Shah Tours specialize in climbs of Kilimanjaro. The Adventure Centre in Arusha (Goliondoi Road) is a mine of safari information.
Local **buses** are not recommended, and *dalla dallas* (privately operated mini-buses) are decidedly dangerous. **Taxis** are available in Arusha and Moshi, where there are also **car hire** firms.

Marangu
Marangu, PO Box 40, Moshi, tel: 900 and ask for Marangu 11, fax: (055) 50639. An old farmhouse in spacious, pleasant gardens with fine views of Kilimanjaro and 35 rooms in a series of cottages around the grounds. Simple, nourishing food, charmingly eccentric with an old-world routine; very relaxing.
Kibo, PO Box 40, Moshi, tel: Marangu 4, fax: (055) 50639. German colonial hotel with lots of character, small but

beautifully exotic gardens, 40 rooms and a dining room serving good, simple food.

Moshi
Most tourists in the Kilimanjaro region stay at Marangu rather than Moshi, although the **Moshi YMCA** is popular with low-budget travellers.

Usa River/Arusha NP area
Dik-Dik Lodge, tel: Usa River 73, fax: (057) 8110/8498. Very popular and well-run hotel in a very pleasant situation. Good food; 18 rooms. **Momela Lodge**, tel: (057) 3038/3798. Situated just outside Arusha NP; 75 rooms. **Mountain Village Lodge**, tel: (057) 2699/2799, fax: (057) 8205. An attractive lodge situated by a pretty crater lake with 42 thatched rondavels, a good restaurant, horse riding, tours of a coffee estate and bird safaris around Lake Duluti. A deservedly popular resort. **Mount Meru Game Lodge**, tel: (057) 7179. Located close to the turn-off to Arusha NP; 15 rooms. **Ngare Sero Mountain Lodge**, tel: Usa River 38. Situated on the lower slopes of Mount Meru with 64 comfortable rooms and homely cuisine. Very good value.

Arusha
Novotel Mount Meru, tel: (057) 2711/2, fax: (057) 8503/8221. Arusha's premier

The Land of Kilimanjaro at a Glance

hotel, with 192 rooms and suites and three restaurants. Recently renovated, though it lacks warmth and intimacy. **Motel Impala**, tel: (057) 8448/51, fax: (057) 8220/8680. Centrally located with 20 rooms. Has its own fleet of safari vehicles with experienced drivers.

Tarangire NP

Tarangire Safari Lodge, tel: (057) 7182. Long-established lodge, well sited on a low escarpment above the Tarangire River. Has 36 spacious, self-contained tents or bungalows and a swimming pool. Extras include game drives.

Tarangire Sopa, enquiries and bookings through Central Reservations Office, Arusha, tel: (057) 6886/6896, fax: (057) 8245. Recently opened luxury lodge with 75 suites, sited 30km (20 miles) from the park entrance. Pleasingly innovative architecture.

Oliver's, tel: (057) 3108. Luxury camp situated just outside the eastern boundary of the National Park.

Mkomazi Game Reserve

There are one or two sparsely furnished huts inside the reserve, but visitors must bring more or less everything they need. In Same town, just outside the reserve, there is the **Elephant Motel**, which has 12 basic but clean and reasonable rooms.

Lushoto

Grant's Lodge, reservations through Rural Development Associates, Tanga; tel: (053) 42491, fax: (053) 43628. The best of the hotels in Lushoto. Lovely gardens and walks and very good home cooking; four rooms.

WHERE TO EAT

Most of the hotels have restaurants; the best are **Dik-Dik** and **Mountain Village** in the Usa River area, **Novotel Mount Meru** and **Impala** in Arusha, and **Ngare Seso** and **Mount Meru Game Lodge** outside Arusha.

TOURS AND EXCURSIONS

The golden rule for short-term visitors to Tanzania is to let the **tour operators** do the organizing (and worrying). For local tours approach one of the many operators to be found in Arusha.

Shorter walks and hikes on Kilimanjaro (eg as far as the first hut)**:** Can be arranged from the National Park gate at Marangu.

Walking on Mount Meru: Can be arranged at either of the entrance gates to Arusha National Park. Guided climbs

to the summit can also be organized (*see* p.55).

Arusha National Park: Most tour companies will oblige; alternatively, self-drive in Arusha NP is fairly straightforward.

Mkomazi Game Reserve: 1–2 hour drive from Moshi, 2–3 from Arusha. Offers big game and lovely sweeping landscapes.

Usambara Mountains: A comfortable 3–4 hour drive from Moshi, 4–5 from Arusha. An **air charter** company in Arusha, Precision Air Services, advertises short flights over both Kilimanjaro and Meru.

USEFUL CONTACTS

Arusha code: 057.
Moshi code: 055.
Emergencies: 999.
Operator: 900.
Tanzanair (Air charter), Dar es salaam: tel: (051) 30232/4.
Air Tanzania, Dar es Salaam: tel: (051) 46643/44111.
Kilimanjaro International Airport: tel: (055) 2223.
Tanzania National Parks HQ, Arusha: tel: (057) 3471/3181.
Tanzania Tourist Board, Arusha: tel: (057) 3842/3, fax: (057) 8256.

KILIMANJARO	J	F	M	A	M	J	J	A	S	O	N	D
AVERAGE TEMP. °F	77	79	77	75	73	70	70	70	72	75	77	77
AVERAGE TEMP. °C	25	26	25	24	23	21	21	21	22	24	25	25
HOURS OF SUN DAILY	10	9	8	6	5	5	5	6	7	8	8	9
RAINFALL ins.	2	2	5	12	6	1	1	1	1	1	2	2
RAINFALL mm	39	44	117	303	157	31	14	14	15	33	55	48
DAYS OF RAINFALL	4	4	8	17	14	5	3	3	3	4	6	6

4
Ngorongoro and the Serengeti

Close to Tarangire, on the Arusha–Dodoma Road, is a small settlement called **Makuyuni**, which means 'The Place of the Fig Tree'. It consists of little more than a filling station, but it has significance. The gravel road which heads across the Rift from Makuyuni takes travellers through **Maasailand,** past **Lake Manyara** and its adjoining National Park, up the steep western wall of the **Rift** and across the rolling, fertile **Mbulu Plateau**. At the southern rim of an extinct volcano one branch of the track descends into the fabulous **Ngorongoro Crater**, while the other travels down to the **Serengeti** plains through the most beautifully soft and sweeping scenery.

The track across those plains can shred tyres, and the country through which it passes can be disappointingly dry and monotonous to the untrained eye and the incurious mind, but if the grass is green and the great migration is passing through, it can live forever in the memory, with streams of wildebeest and zebra soft-focussed in the mists beneath Makarut, or cantering across the sunlit savanna under Naabi Hill.

THE RIFT VALLEY

The gravel track which crosses the Rift Valley is ribbed with corrugations, which can shake a vehicle and its passengers down to their respective chassis. In the dry season it is dusty, in the rains it can flood. The Rift itself was formed as continental drift tore East Africa apart, dropping in a series of blocks along parallel fault lines,

CLIMATE

Daytime temperatures can rise quite high, even in Ngorongoro, but mean temperatures fall between 15°C (59°F) and 25°C (77°F). During the dry season (May to October) nights and early mornings can be cold enough for log fires to be lit in the lodges. Humidity is relatively low. The wettest months are usually March and April, when travel can sometimes be difficult on certain tracks.

Opposite: *Migrating wildebeest take the plunge at the Mara River.*

DON'T MISS

*** Ngorongoro Crater: world famous 'bowl' of wildlife. Best place to see rhino in Tanzania.
*** Serengeti migration: at its best in December and January, when the herds are in the southern plains and weather conditions are usually favourable.
** Lake Manyara National Park: fine setting, with elephants, tree-climbing lions and flamingoes.
* Olduvai Gorge: site of Louis and Mary Leakeys' famous archeological finds.

Opposite: *Once much feared, now much photographed – the proud and colourful warriors of Maasailand.*

and resulting eventually in a system of irregular valleys, which stretches from the Dead Sea to Mozambique.

Parts of the Rift, especially by Ol Doinyo Lengai, ('Mountain of God' to the Maasai) have a hard, spare beauty, founded on geological violence. Lengai itself remains violent – it rises, just outside the northeastern corner of the Ngorongoro Conservation Unit in a steep cone to 2678m (8785ft). In 1966 it blew its main vent, spewing a plume of gas and cinders 1500m (5000ft) into the air, and coating the mountain and the downwind plains with a snow-fall of caustic ash. It overlooks the bitter, pink and plum-coloured waters of **Lake Natron**, one of the Rift's string of alkaline lakes, and a breeding ground of the lesser flamingo.

The Maasai

The Rift is Maasai country. Tourists travelling down the road to Mto-Wa-Mbu, a little settlement across the Valley under the western Rift wall, will see the Maasai and their God-given cattle, as well as *enkang*, the circular arrangements of huts where the families and their cattle live. *Murran* (more commonly *moran*), the young warriors, live in their own *manyattas* elsewhere, with some of the *ndito* – the unmarried girls.

The Maasai have been much admired and romanticized. They are a fascinating people, many of whom cling to a traditional lifestyle. The men wear red blankets draped over their shoulders, carry spears or sticks and cover their hair and bodies with sheepfat and ochre. Livestock are central to their lives, and their diet

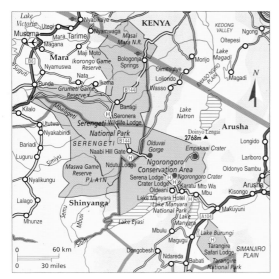

still includes cow's blood mixed with milk. They appear to be at one with their environment, but life is still harsh: traditionally children often have two lower incisors knocked out to allow feeding in the event of lock-jaw, and male and female circumcision is still carried out without anaesthetic (*see* p. 25). Maasai are not, however, unaffected by tourism, and tourists wanting to photograph them can expect to pay for the privilege.

Lake Manyara National Park ★★

Mto Wa Mbu (Mosquito River) is well named, and well-situated. The little settlement has become a temporary stop-over for tourists and campers, providing them with souvenirs (mostly rather tacky), fuel and basic groceries. Its population is tribally mixed. Just beyond the township, to the south, is Lake Manyara National Park, between the lake and the Rift wall.

The 330km² (127 sq miles) Manyara National Park was once known for its **elephants**, **rhino** and its **tree-climbing lions,** as well as the **flamingoes** and other fascinating **birds** which can be seen in impressive numbers on and around the shallow, alkaline lake. The area was once famous among big game hunters (one of them, Ernest Hemingway, describes it in *The Green Hills of Africa*). The

---

MAASAI HUTS

Travellers across the Rift will see the circular *enkang* or family settlements of the Maasai, sometimes surrounded by a barrier of euphorbia or thorn trees, which keep cattle in and leopards and lions out. The low, loaf-shaped huts, built by the women from saplings and waterproof coverings of cow-dung are traditionally divided, by a screen, into two rooms, with a convoluted entrance hall between. Calves or goats are sometimes housed in this hallway at night. The main herds spend the night in the centre of the *enkang*, surrounded by their own little stockade. Each hut in an *enkang* has a special place, according to the status of its occupants.

THE LERAI FOREST

One of the most noticeable features of Ngorongoro Crater, when seen from the rim, is the Lerai Forest. Its name derives from the Maasai word for the yellow-bark acacia trees, which were once called 'fever trees' – a matter of guilt by association, for they grow in damp habitats, often alongside standing water, which of course is a wonderful breeding ground for the anopheles mosquito. The Lerai sometimes harbours bull elephant and waterbuck, but less than 30 years ago 23 rhino were resident in the forest, an amazing density of 7 rhino to the square kilometre (19 to the square mile). Other major features of the Crater include Lake Makat (the name means 'soda' in Maasai), the Mandusi and Gorigor swamps, and Engitate Hill.

elephant suffered drastically from the highly organized poaching of the 1980s, but are now quickly recovering, unlike the rhino. The lion, and the acacia trees in which they sometimes rest, remain.

Visitors often rush through Manyara's gloomy **ground-water forest,** the lovely *acacia tortilis* **woodland** and along the **soda flats** of its lake, before driving on to lunch at Ngorongoro. Yet Manyara has so much to offer to those who can afford to stay for a day or more; one geologically interesting attraction is the **hot spring** at the far end of the park.

NGORONGORO CRATER

From Manyara the road makes a steep ascent up the Rift Wall (don't miss the fine views from the little lay-by near the top). The track then crosses the rolling **Mbulu Plateau**, rich farming country tilled by the Mbulu people (more properly the Iraqw). Beyond this lies the steep, thickly-forested side of the Ngorongoro Crater, arguably the most famous wildlife refuge in the world. From the lodges on the crater rim, at about 2400m (8000ft), you look down upon the near-circular crater floor, an expanse of flat, open grassland, forest and lake 14km (9 miles) across. Around it stands a ring of extinct volcanoes with poetic Maasai names, and within the beautiful

Left: *Lake Makat (the Maasai word meaning soda) on the floor of Ngorongoro Crater.* **Opposite:** *A chance to relax by the swimming pool of Lake Manyara Hotel, overlooking the Rift Valley.*

irregularity of the bowl, something like 20,000 large or moderately large animals live out their lives. The crater (more accurately caldera) is a remarkable natural amphitheatre which properly takes its place as one of the essential highlights of East Africa.

The crater once belonged to the Maasai. In 1958 they signed away their right to live there, though they still take their cattle down to the soda-licks around Lake Makat. Sometimes they can still be seen, striding across their old pastures with their herds, raising the dust of history as well as the volcanic soil. Red shukas streaming in the breeze, spears gleaming in the sun, they make a fine and moving sight.

Earlier in the 20th century the crater was occupied by German (and later British) farmers and squatters. In 1954 the squatters were evicted, and in 1959 the Conservation Area was inaugurated.

Visitors to Ngorongoro commonly arrive at one of the lodges after a day's trip from Arusha and Lake Manyara. The next morning they descend into the crater, 600m (2000ft) below, a volcanic basin where, despite the prevailing atmosphere of tranquillity, an abundance of animals jostle for a place in an intricately poised struggle for survival. In many ways the crater provides its tenants

FARMERS IN EDEN

In the early years of the 20th century two German brothers, **Friedrich and Adolph Siedentopf**, farmed the fabulous Ngorongoro Crater. The ruins of both farms can still be seen, one behind the Lerai Forest and the other across the crater on the slopes above the Munge Stream. They and their cattle shared the land with the **Maasai**, and of course some pretty eclectic farm animals, such as rhino and elephant. The Maasai, who believe that they own all the cattle in the world, sometimes 'claimed back' a few German beasts, and lion, which were often shot on sight as vermin, took a few more. The outbreak of World War I forced the brothers to leave Ngorongoro.

RHINO ROMEOS AND OTHER STRANGE AFFAIRS

● **Rhino** numbers are at endangered levels, but when boy *does* meet girl, they make the most of it – copulation can last up to an hour.
● Moral and genetic problems over incestuous relationships in the confines of the Crater do not trouble the **lions**, as mating seems to be one of their main preoccupations. Lionesses need repetitive sexual stimulation before they ovulate, which keeps the handsome and often black-maned lions of Ngorongoro fairly busy.
● Female **hyenas** have taken feminism to fascinating extremes – they are larger and more dominant than males, and are equipped with identical sexual organs (in terms of size and shape, even when erect). Although they are not hermaphrodite, the male hyena, when his fancy turns to thoughts of love, is confronted by a partner exactly like himself but bigger, which cannot be all that good for the ego.

with their every need, but the rent in paradise can be very high, and is often paid in blood. Ngorongoro is not the open zoo that it sometimes seems to be; the animals are wild, and some can be dangerous. It is well to remember this.

The Wildlife

The numbers of **lion** on the crater floor varies, but is often around 100. Because of the nature of the crater, and the abundance of food, there is little pressure on the lions to move out, and much resistance to lions trying to move in. Consequently, many of Ngorongoro's lions are said to be closely related, which might (or might not) prove genetically damaging.

Lion are always popular, but the animal most tourists hope to to see in the crater is the **black rhino**, as Ngorongoro is one of the few places left in Africa where this much-persecuted creature can be seen in the wild. In the mid-1960s the biologist John Goddard recorded 110 rhinos on the crater floor. These were reduced to about 10 or 12 by the poaching epidemic of the 1980s. Since then, numbers in the crater have increased to about 20, thanks to more effective protection, though repopulation is slow, with gestation alone averaging 15 months.

Right: *A bull elephant reminds safari companies that he has right of way in Ngorongoro Crater.*
Opposite: *A vehicle negotiates the steep and winding ascent road out of Ngorongoro Crater.*

Another much-maligned animal in Ngorongoro is the **spotted hyena**. Like lion, hyena are largely active at night, and are great opportunists. Contrary to former opinion, however, they are very efficient hunters, and in Ngorongoro the image of the cowardly, skulking scavenger has been finally laid to rest. There are about eight clans living in Ngorongoro in their respective territories across the crater floor, each clan composed of 10 to 100 members. They are capable of keeping up a near-tireless, loping run, and of bringing down prey as large as adult wildebeest and zebra. Hyena kill about one quarter of all the new-born wildebeest in the crater each year, and are responsible for more overall kills than the lions, which, ironically, scavenge from the hyena.

Ngorongoro teems with other interesting species and in the crater there is rarely a dull moment. There seem to be animals everywhere – **elephant**, **wildebeest**, **zebra**, **buffalo**, **eland**, **Grant's** and **Thomson's gazelle**, **warthog** and many others, including the leggy and attractively spotted **serval cat** which patrols the taller grasslands, pouncing on mice or leaping from cover to claw birds from the air. The crater floor is perfect for **larks, long-claws**, **pipits** and **plovers**, as it is for the much larger **ostriches**, **Kori bustards** and the elegant **crowned cranes**.

NOT JUST THE CRATER

The Crater is only a small part of the Ngorongoro Conservation Area, 8300km^2 (3200 sq miles) in extent, and a unique experiment in multiple land-use. Its main features are the Crater Highlands (of which the famous crater is a small part) and the short-grass plains beyond, which merge with the vast grasslands of the adjacent Serengeti National Park.

Wildlife is protected throughout the area, with elephant, buffalo, leopard, bushbuck and a host of other animals being present, sometimes surprisingly close to the lodges on the crater's edge. Birds are abundant along the forested rim, and in and around the lodge gardens.

Above: *Olduvai Gorge,*
the site of many exciting
palaentological discoveries.

IN THE MIDST OF
DEATH – LIFE

There is life in Olduvai, as
well as relics of death. On
the rocks, visitors will see
large Agama lizards, with
orange-red heads and blue
bodies (they turn grey when
threatened and trying to
hide). And there are many
interesting birds, some of
them quite 'tame'. Plants in
and around the Gorge include
the wild sisal, after which
Olduvai was named, and
the 'wait-a-bit thorn', *Acacia*
mellifera. Its common name
will become quickly apparent
to visitors who brush against
it and find themselves caught
up in a complex of recurved
thorns. The area isn't devoid
of game either, and lion and
cheetah are sometimes found
resting in the thickets.

Olduvai Gorge *

Ngorongoro Crater has its share of archeological sites,
and at least one splendid and sacred fig tree, said to
be planted over the body of a Barabaig warrior chief.
But the track which passes between the crater rim
and the slopes of Oldeani, the 'Mountain of Bamboo',
then curves down towards the Serengeti, eventually
crossing a slight but famous rocky gorge, where history
has literally been laid bare.

In 1931 **Dr Louis Leakey**, following up previous
explorations of Olduvai by a German professor, found
human remains here. In 1959, after almost three decades
of unrelenting work, Louis' wife **Mary** came running
back to camp crying 'I've got him! I've got him!' The
gentleman in question was nearly 2 million years old,
and Mary had uncovered fragments of his skull.
She named him 'Nutcracker Man' (*Australopithacus*
boisei). Remains of 'Handy Man' (*Homo habilis*) – also
about 1.8 million years old – were found later.

An even more exciting find came in 1976, when Mary
Leakey discovered, in petrified volcanic ash at **Laetoli**,
some 20km (12 miles) south of Olduvai, the clearly pre-
served footprints of three hominids. One was relatively
large – though no more than 1.4m (4ft 7in), one medium-
sized, and one small: perhaps a man, woman and child,

if such terms are appropriate for hominids with a brain less than one third the size of our own. Whatever they were, they walked upright, and their stroll took place 3.5 million years ago.

There is a visitors' centre at Olduvai, with an interesting little museum and guided tours of the immediate gorge for those who choose to take them. Unless visitors are particularly interested, an hour in the vicinity is long enough.

SERENGETI NATIONAL PARK

Both Olduvai and Laetoli are on the edge of the Serengeti, 'The Great Open Place' to the Maasai. The Maasai lost the Serengeti, along with Ngorongoro, when the areas were made into National Parks, but at places such as the Bell Rock at **Moru Kopjes**, where the impact of a large rock being struck by smaller ones rings out across the great plains, there is evidence of the warriors' passing. Rangers will tell you that the *Il murran* would strike the rock to guide their cattle-raiding comrades home, but knowing the warriors, they probably did it just to amuse themselves. There is a cave nearby, where warriors would sleep, with rock-paintings of Maasai shields and figures by its entrance.

SERENGETI KOPJES

Kopje (pronounced copy) is a Dutch word meaning small hill. The Serengeti kopjes consist of old granite rock, broken and worn by constant expansion and contraction due to abrupt temperature changes. Like oceanic islands, they have their own range of vegetation and wildlife, and are often home to lizards, hyrax and those delightful antelopes, the dik-dik. Snakes such as the spitting cobra are sometimes found there, as are klipspringer antelope, lion and leopard. Close to the Naabi Hill–Seronera track and about 10km (6 miles) to the southeast of Seronera are the Simba Kopjes, always worth a visit, as are the Maasai Kopjes near Seronera itself. The Moru Kopjes are some 30km (20 miles) south of Seronera, and a pleasant place to spend the day, and enjoy a picnic lunch, or even camp.

Left: *Plain sailing – a balloon drifts silently over the short-grass savanna of the Serengeti.*

BLACK-MANED LIONS

Male lions in Ngorongoro and the Serengeti often have beautiful black manes, once much-prized by hunters. As a leonine means of showing off, bushy black manes, like bushy black beards, have their advantages, but when hunting on open grassland, an approaching black hay-stack must look as obvious, to a wildebeest or zebra, as a London taxi. Which might explain why female lions everywhere do most of the hunting and why, especially in the Crater, most lion scavenge from hyena in any case.

Kopjes – outcrops of granite rock – rise like shimmering islands in the Serengeti's sea of grass, and are a most attractive feature of the Park. One of them, **Naabi Hill,** marks the major gate of the Serengeti, commanding the most beautiful acacia and short-grass savanna, the plains sweeping away on every hand as if to challenge the concept of the horizon.

Big Cats

The Serengeti is ideal **cheetah** habitat. The fastest mammal on Earth needs a firm and reliable running track and space in which to manoeuvre. The short-grass plains provide both. The grasslands are also dotted with Thomson's and Grant's gazelle, the most common prey for these fast-moving cats.

Lions enjoy the Serengeti too, as one might expect in what for them must seem like the biggest supermarket on earth, with no-one manning the tills. And that other charismatic and exquisite feline, the **leopard**, is common, though not necessarily commonly seen. More nocturnal and shy than lions and cheetahs, the leopard can sometimes be found along the Seronera Valley, in the centre of the Park, along other water-courses, or among the kopjes. Leopard are attracted to bait at some of the Kenyan safari lodges, but in Tanzania the purists pretend to be offended by such chicanery.

Left: *Wildebeest hard at work mowing the Serengeti plains.*
Opposite: *A female cheetah with four young mouths to feed, scans the Musiara Plains.*

The Serengeti Migration

For the resident lion and spotted hyena, however, life is largely feast or famine, as the convenience food on which they rely so much, wildebeest and zebra, have a disconcerting habit of disappearing. However, what is frustrating for the cats is pure theatre for tourists, and the Serengeti migration can well claim to be the greatest wildlife show on Earth.

Involving huge numbers of animals in a spectacular landscape, the migration is, at its best, almost overwhelming in its visual and emotional impact. The sanctuary in which it takes place is 14,763km² (5700 sq miles) in area, as big as Northern Ireland. It is adjoined by the **Masai Mara** across the border, **Maswa Game Reserve** to the west, **Ngorongoro Conservation Area** to the southeast and **Loliondo Controlled Area** to the east. Two smaller controlled areas lie to the northwest. Even by African standards, this is game country on a vast scale.

The animals involved in the migration move because they need to eat. Two million or more herbivores need a lot of grass, and in the long dry season, from May to November, the short-grass plains south and southeast of Seronera are dessicated (and in any case shorn as short

MIGRATION FACT FILE

● As many as 1,500,000 wildebeest and 200,000 zebra take part in the journey, augmented by throngs of semi-migratory Thomson's gazelle, eland, topi and hartebeest. There can be densities of 500 wildebeest per square kilometre.
● To add to the turmoil, the beginning of the trek, in May or June, coincides with the wildebeest rutting period.
● The herds are constantly under threat from a variety of predators, including 1500 lion, 4000 hyena, 500 cheetah, as well as leopard and wild dog. Many hyena actually commute, for distances of up to 60km (40 miles) or more, from their home bases, to find prey.
● In length, the journey from the short-grass plains and back again is 800km (500 miles).

WHEN TO SEE THE MIGRATION

• The best time to see the migration is probably during **January** and **February**, when weather conditions are usually good and there are heavy concentrations of animals in the southern-most regions of the park. Convenient lodges are Seronera, Serengeti Serena, Serengeti Sopa and Lake Ndutu Tented Camp.

• During the dry season from **June to November**, the big concentrations of game are often in the west or north. Lodges in these areas include Grumeti River and Kirawira (west), and Lobo and Migration (north).

• While the migration is, of course, the Serengeti's greatest draw, it is still a vast area of beautiful African landscape, and a good number of animals (especially the predators) can be seen throughout the year.

as lawns by two million sets of incisors). So at the end of May or in early June (the timing varies, depending on the rains) the greatest natural circus in the world gets on the road. Its performers move out in files which can be 40km (25 miles) long, and the short-grass plains are sometimes virtually emptied of migratory animals within three or four days. It is this brief and unpredictable exodus which is so often filmed and photographed by those lucky enough to be around at the time.

The herds are followed, at least for some of the way, by the more nomadic predators – certain lions, hyenas and jackals. The long journey also takes the migrant herds through the home ranges of prides of lion and packs of hyena, and across rivers, such as the **Grumeti** and the **Mara**, where monstrous crocodiles lie in wait, to fling themselves upon drinking animals or twist great chunks from the corpses of those that drown.

The hazardous journey takes the herds out into the **Western Corridor** of the Serengeti, then far beyond the Kenyan border, before returning to the southern plains. It is a triangular trek of about 800km (500 miles) which some wildebeest will complete many times before disease or predators catch up with them, a testimony to their toughness. Surprisingly, however, an adult

wildebeest can be brought down by a lion, or even a single hyena, with scarcely a groan of protest, despite its size and horns, though a female will often successfully defend her young against similar attacks.

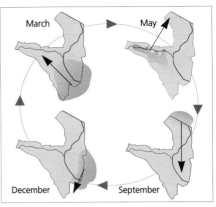

THE SERENGETI WILDEBEEST MIGRATION CYCLE

The **return** to the short-grass plains is timed to coincide with the Short Rains in December, and with the short and synchronized calving season which usually begins in January. Sometimes they (or the Gods) get it wrong: if the rains come late, or not at all, up to 80% of the new calves die due to lack of food. When they get it right, the scenes on the short-grass, with hundreds of thousands of animals scattered across a whole landscape, and the calves skipping, running and bleating with apparent *joie de vivre*, are almost as spectacular as the exodus in May or June. And, of course, the timing is more convenient for tourists.

The wildebeests' travelling companions include large numbers of their antelope cousins, the **topi** and the **hartebeest** (*kongoni*). Their hind legs, shorter than the fore, act like low gears, to give them maximum acceleration from a standing start, and once on the move they are soon in overdrive. They are among the fastest of herbivores and, despite their ungainly shape, quite attractive.

Smaller Animals

One of the Serengeti's more interesting residents is the **honey-badger** – loose-skinned, powerfully jawed and, when aroused, utterly fearless. Their silver-grey and black coloration is for warning, not camouflage, and honey-badgers (sometimes called *ratels*) will attack animals as large as buffalo, biting the groin and genital organs and leaving the animal to bleed to death. Tourists needn't walk around in body armour, however, although the honey-badger has been known to attack car tyres.

DEFENDING WILDEBEEST

Wildebeest are not the clowns of the plains they are sometimes said to be. Nature hasn't blessed them with a high IQ but they are otherwise well-adapted to a lifestyle which, in human terms, no insurance company would touch. A calf can stand almost as soon as it is born, and within an average time of seven minutes is able to run, albeit unsteadily, for its life. With a range of hungry predators on their tail, such precocity is very much in their interest. The wildebeest's lawnmower of a mouth is superbly designed to harvest grass – which is why they eat themselves out of house and home twice a year, and why they migrate.

Opposite: *A resting leopard lounges in the limbs of an acacia.*

Right: *A klipspringer, the 'Goat of the Rocks', watches from a Serengeti kopje.*
Opposite: *Thompson's gazelle, distinguished by a black side stripe, on the Serengeti plains.*

Other smaller mammals of the Serengeti include the **black** or **silver-backed jackal**, **golden jackal**, **bat-eared fox**, **genet** (often to be seen around Ndutu Lodge), six species of **mongoose** and the skunk-like **zorilla**. Altogether there are almost 100 species of mammal found in the Park, and nearly 500 **birds**. Ground-nesting birds are abundant in the short-grass plains, as are the storks, vultures, eagles, hawks and falcons which thrive on the prodigality of the grasslands.

Around the Park

The short-grass plains of the southeastern Serengeti phase into an intermediate zone by **Naabi Hill**, and into long-grass plains closer to **Seronera**, where the Park Headquarters, a lodge and a research institute are situated. About 18km (11 miles) north of Seronera is Banagi, and just to the east of here is **Kilimafedha**, the 'Hill of Wealth', so-called because gold was mined here until 1966. The gold-bearing quartz is embedded in some of the most ancient rock on Earth, found between Banagi and Kilimafedha, and some two to three thousand million years old. The Serengeti is not short on superlatives.

SWEET-TALKING BIRD

The myopic and misanthropic honey-badger has a remarkable relationship with the honey guide (the Latin name of which is – appropriately – *Indicator indicator*). The honey guide is a small bird which attracts the badger (and human honey-hunters) to wild bees' nests by its behaviour and calls. The badger then digs out the nest, and bird and mammal share the spoils. The bird gets the best of the deal – the honey-badger is, in fact, quite capable of finding its own hives.

Towards **Banagi**, and northwards towards the Kenya border, the country lifts into rolling uplands, fledged with bush and patchy woodland, relieved by open areas and ranges of hills. Many of the hills have crumbled into magnificent kopjes, and among the granite boulders of Lobo Hill, a most imaginatively sited lodge is tucked away. The country in this vicinity is a joy to eye and soul, and from August to November part of the great migration passes through, adding spectacle to splendour.

Another interesting area of the Serengeti is the **Western Corridor**, a tapering arm of the park which stretches to **Ndabaka Gate**, overlooking the shores of Lake Victoria. It is at its best, as far as game viewing is concerned, during the dry season from June to October. This is also the best time for travelling, as there are extensive black-cotton grasslands 30km (20 miles) east of Ndabaka. Black-cotton soil can be a nightmare during the rains, even for experienced off-the-road drivers in four-wheel-drive vehicles, and in the bush, discretion is almost always the better part of valour.

GRUMETI RIVER

The main feature of the Western Corridor is the Grumeti River, which flows through the Corridor from east to west, and empties into Lake Victoria. Exceptionally large crocodiles live in this river, and visitors are advised not to stand or walk too close to the water's edge, for the huge reptiles are capable of surging from the river to grab unsuspecting wildebeest (or unsuspecting tourists). The less violent and extremely attractive colobus monkey lives in the canopy of the riverine forest, and that other magnificent black and white creature, the martial eagle, can sometimes be seen in the area.

Ngorongoro and Serengeti at a Glance

BEST TIMES TO VISIT

The period of the Long Rains (mid-March to mid-May) and occasionally the Short Rains (mid-October to mid-December) can be frustrating or dismal, and some park tracks at these times can be difficult or impassable. The months from **mid-May** to **mid-October** are normally dry but cool after dark. The migration is in the southern Serengeti from **mid December to mid-March**.

GETTING THERE

Most visitors to Ngorongoro and Serengeti travel by **road** from Arusha. Almost everyone takes advantage of the many safari **tour operators** in Arusha, although car hire is available in Arusha, and some tourists **fly** in through private charter companies, also based in Arusha. It is possible to get to Lake Manyara, and to Ngorongoro, by **bus** from Arusha, but it is not the ideal way to travel.

GETTING AROUND

Most people travel on **package tours** or independently by **car**. However, most lodges in the parks operate game-viewing tours in their own four-wheel-drive vehicles.

WHERE TO STAY

Lake Manyara Area
Gibbs Farm, tel: 900 and ask for Karatu 25, fax: (057) 8310. Head office, Arusha, tel: (057) 6702, fax: (057) 8310. Small but very attractive old farm with 15 double rooms. Good wholesome home cooking and excellent local coffee.
Kirurumo Tented Lodge, contact Hoopoe Tours, tel: (057) 7011. Newly opened camp on edge of escarpment overlooking Lake Manyara with 30 self-contained tents.
Lake Manyara Hotel, tel: (057) 8802. Head office, Arusha, tel: (057) 3842/3843. Long-established but no longer superior hotel on edge of escarpment with100 self-contained rooms, swimming pool and restaurant.
Lake Manyara Serena Lodge, contact Serena Central Reservations in Arusha, tel: (057) 8175/6304, fax: (057) 8282. Dramatic setting on the edge of the Rift escarpment overlooking Lake Manyara. Designed on theme of an African village; 66 rooms.
Maji Moto Camp, contact Archer's Tours, tel: Nairobi (254-2) 23131/331825, fax: (254-2) 340182. Exclusive tented camp, and the only tourist resort actually inside Lake Manyara National Park. Situated by the Hot Springs, with the Rift Wall as a backdrop. Game drives, good food, personalized service, privacy and comfort.

Ngorongoro Area
Ngorongoro Crater Lodge, controlled by the South African Conservation Corporation, tel: (057) 3303, fax: (057) 8268. Oldest of the crater rim lodges (1934), though it seems even older, with a rustic, 'early settler' atmosphere. Expensive but beautifully situated, and a favourite with Ngorongoro connoisseurs.
Ngorongoro Serena Lodge, contact Serena Central Reservations (see Lake Manyara Serena Lodge). Recently built on the crater rim, it offers unhindered views of the crater floor, despite being scarcely visible from below. Lives up to the high standards of the Serena hotels; 75 rooms.
Ngorongoro Sopa Lodge, contact Sopa Central Reservations Office, Arusha, tel: (057) 6886/6896, fax: (057) 8254. Luxury lodge, on the eastern edge of crater with 100 suites , a good restaurants offering vegetarian and African dishes, swimming pool, enclosed solariums, satellite TV and videos.
Ngorongoro Wildlife Lodge, tel: (057) 8150/2404. Head office, Arusha, tel: (057) 3842/3843. Long-established, beautifully situated on the southern rim of crater. Has 75 centrally heated rooms, a reasonable restaurant and lounge with log fires.

Serengeti
Grumeti River Camp, contact Archer's Tours (see Maji Moto Camp). An exclusive

tented camp with 10 luxury tents and a swimming pool. Camp has its own safari vehicles and game drives and guided walking safaris along the river are organized. Privacy, comfort, attentive personalized service and very good food.
Kirawira Camp, contact Serena Central Reservations (*see* Lake Manyara Serona Lodge). Luxury tented camp situated on a hill by the Grumeti River in the western corridor of the park. Part of the Serena chain.
Lobo Lodge, tel: (057) 3842/3843. Long-established though no longer the best, but beautifully situated among the boulders of a kopje in the northern section of park. Recently refurbished; 75 rooms, swimming pool.
Migration Camp, tel: (051) 36134/36138, fax: (051) 36107. Recently opened luxury tented camp, cleverly concealed among the granite rocks of the Ndassiata Hills near Lobo in the north of the park. Sun-deck, swimming pool, viewing platforms overlooking the Grumeti River, conducted walking safaris and balloon flights arranged.
Ndutu Safari Lodge, tel: (057) 6702/8930, fax: (057) 8310. A long-established lodge situated just outside the southern border of the Serengeti by Lake Ndutu with 32 double rooms and six double tents.

Serengeti Sopa, contact Sopa Central Reservations (*see* Ngorongoro Sopa Lodge). Luxury lodge of 100 suites. with floor to ceiling glass doors overlooking the Serengeti Plains. Swimming pool, very good restaurants with imaginative cuisine.
Seronera Lodge, tel: (057) 3842/3843. Long-established and recently refurbished though no longer top of the range. Has 75 self-contained rooms built among the rocks of a kopje in the centre of the park, in an area famous for its lion, leopard and cheetah. Popular and often, from a wildlife point of view, very rewarding.

WHERE TO EAT

As a general rule you will eat where you stay, but if you have the time and opportunity you should have at least one picnic lunch or breakfast out in the bush. It's a wonderful experience, and most lodges will oblige.

TOURS AND EXCURSIONS

Empakai Crater: Makes an interesting diversion for visitors to Ngorongoro; more adventurous visitors might want to go down into the Rift to the beautifully wild area around the active volcano Ol Doinyo Lengai.
Olduvai Gorge: Famous prehistoric site where the Leakey family discovered 'Nutcracker Man' and 'Handy Man' and where many other interesting remains have been unearthed. There is a small museum and guided tours of some of the more important sites.
Balloon safaris: Operated from Seronera Lodge but are open to visitors from other lodges. They are expensive but offer a once-in-a-lifetime flight of fancy above one of the most famous national parks in the world. Includes champagne breakfast. The adventure begins about 06:00 and you return to Seronera Lodge about 09:15.

USEFUL CONTACTS

Arusha code: 057.
Emergencies: 999.
Operator: 900.
Kilimanjaro International Airport: tel: (055) 2223.
Tanzania National Parks HQ, Arusha: tel: (057) 3471/3181.
Tanzania Tourist Board, Arusha: tel: (057) 3842/3, fax: (057) 8256.

NGORONGORO	J	F	M	A	M	J	J	A	S	O	N	D
AVERAGE TEMP. °F	70	70	70	70	66	63	63	64	66	68	70	70
AVERAGE TEMP. °C	21	21	21	21	19	17	17	18	19	20	21	21
HOURS OF SUN DAILY	8	8	7	6	6	5	6	7	8	9	8	7
RAINFALL ins.	3	3	5	10	3	1	0	0	0	1	4	4
RAINFALL mm	74	85	139	245	78	18	9	7	10	20	107	96
DAYS OF RAINFALL	9	9	13	21	13	4	3	2	2	2	10	11

5
The Lakes

It is difficult for most of us today to appreciate the fascination which the 'question of the Nile' held for the geographers, politicians and the better-informed general public of Victorian Britain. Explorers and missionaries tramped westwards from the east coast of Africa to the Lakes in search of the source of the sacred river and, perhaps, some kind of immortality. They mostly found mortality. Even Livingstone was brought to his knees, and an early death, in the swamps of Bangweulu (now in northern Zambia), hopelessly seduced by the search for those elusive headwaters. And the man who finally solved the nagging question, John Hanning Speke, shot himself soon afterwards and is now almost forgotten.

The answer they all sought was that the Nile flows from the lake which is still called **Victoria**, the name chosen by Speke in 1858. Known by the Luo people of Kenya as *Nam Lolwe*, 'Lake Without End', Victoria is almost 70,000km² (27,000 sq miles) in area, the biggest lake in Africa and the second largest in the world.

Tanzania shares Lake Victoria with Kenya and Uganda, and **Lake Tanganyika**, 320km (200 miles) to the southwest, with Zaïre. Tanganyika, unlike Victoria, is a Rift Valley lake, and at more than 1433m (4700ft) is the second deepest in the world. It is also the world's longest freshwater lake. In the southwestern corner of the country is the third great lake, **Malawi**. Shared with both Malawi and Mozambique, it is another Rift Valley lake, overlooked by the magnificent Livingstone Mountains.

CLIMATE

The climate around the Lakes is very similar, in some respects, to that at the coast. The atmosphere can be oppressively hot and humid during the single rainy season, from the beginning of November to end of April, but generally the lakes themselves have a cooling effect, and temperatures are normally pleasant and constant. Minimum temperatures at Mwanza throughout the year are about 17°C (62°F) with maximums of 28°C (82°F).

Opposite: *Canoes on Lake Tanganyika, a ready way to sell fresh produce.*

DON'T MISS

The Lakes are generally undeveloped for tourism at present. Visitors will need to allow more time than normal, and perhaps to expect more discomfort.
*** Gombe Stream National Park: chimpanzee refuge and site of well-known research by Dr Jane Goodall.
** Mahale Mountains National Park: also a chimp refuge, but harder to get to.
* Mwanza: restful little town on shores of Lake Victoria. Ferry runs across lake to Bukoba on western shore.
* Ujiji: where H.M. Stanley met Livingstone. A memorial marks the spot, although there is little else.
* Lake Malawi: boat trips under the steep face of the Livingstone Mountains.

Below: *The pleasant town of Mwanza, on the shores of Lake Victoria.*

LAKE VICTORIA

John Speke first saw the lake he was to call Victoria on 3 August 1858, from a point where the town of **Mwanza** now stands. Speke was wondrously confident that he was looking at the lake which fed the Nile, and in memory of his momentous sighting the inlet he had been standing beside was later named Speke's Gulf.

The country through which he had marched from **Kazeh**, close to present-day **Tabora**, is largely unremarkable until the traveller approaches the lake, when the monotonous landscape is transformed into sweeping, almost treeless plains which are studded like the Serengeti with islands of granite. The air grows more humid and the land greener, for Victoria has its own micro-climate, and moods. Its shallow, normally placid waters tend to reflect the hues of the sky, and during storms its colour can almost match the blackness of its temper. On calm, fine days it glitters with a scintillating blueness, and its sunsets, from the eastern shores, can be astonishing in their reflected intensity. The writer Alan Moorehead has said that such scenes 'are very beautiful, and yet there is a mysterious and disturbing atmosphere about the lake. One feels here very strongly the primitiveness of Africa, its overwhelming multiplicity in emptiness'.

Mwanza *

Mwanza, on Lake Victoria's southeastern corner, is a pleasant enough place, especially along its waterfront, without being particularly vibrant or noteworthy. For those who just want to relax, its air of unreproving indolence, broken only by the cries of the hadada ibis which roosts in the lakeside trees, can be a virtue in itself.

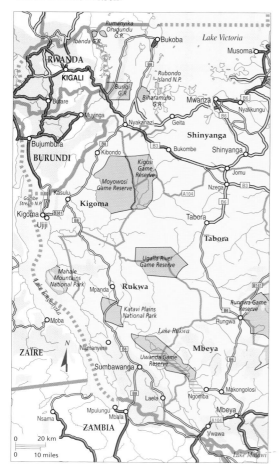

VICTORIA'S FISH

Lake Victoria teems with life, although there are ecological worries about the depletion of fish stocks and the threat of pollution. **Bilharzia** is a potent threat, and algae and weeds are choking the water and killing the **Nile Perch**, introduced to provide a food source but which proceeded to eat all the endemic fish that kept the algae at bay. Even so, Victoria yields 500 tonnes of fish annually, more than 25% of all Africa's freshwater harvests.

BURTON AND SPEKE

Richard Burton and John Hanning Speke had little in common but their ambition to discover the source of the Nile. Setting out in 1856 they had expected to find only one great lake. On the trip, Speke went temporarily blind, and Burton's health broke down completely. While the Irishman was recovering in Kazeh, near Tabora, Speke travelled north and became the first European to see the lake he named Victoria. Two years later Speke returned and saw the outflow of the Nile at Ripon Falls (in present-day Uganda). Speke's claims were doubted, especially by Burton, and on the eve of a debate on the issue between the two former companions in England, Speke shot himself while out hunting partridge. Many assumed that it was suicide.

THE AMPHIBIOUS SITATUNGA

The sitatunga resembles a long-legged bushbuck, but with fairly long, shaggy hair which is slightly oily, enabling them to spend much of their time in the water, or even completely immersed when threatened. Their splayed hooves allow them to step more easily across spongy mats of vegetation. On dry land, however, the hooves are something of a hindrance, making the animal more vulnerable to predators or hunters, though the sitatunga, like the bushbuck, will defend itself courageously against attackers, including men and dogs.

Mwanza's economy in recent years has largely depended upon the agricultural produce of its fertile hinterland, farmed mostly by the dominant tribe of the area, the **Sukuma**. The Sukuma are growers of cotton, maize and cassava, and they also herd cattle, although the coffee shipped through the port originates in the West Lake Province, across the waters.

A short ferry trip from Mwanza is **Saa Nane** (Two O'Clock) Island. It boasts a small wildlife sanctuary, a few interesting birds and some attractive scenery. A picnic on the island can be a very enjoyable way of spending the afternoon. Mwanza's best-known landmark, **Bismark's Rock**, can be seen from the ferry, just offshore from the town.

Rubondo *

Another, much bigger island, and of much greater interest in terms of wildlife, is Rubondo, in the south-western corner of Lake Victoria. It is not an easy place to get to, but for the more adventurous travellers it is worth the time and effort, for it is a National Park with a difference. Its humid forest and wetland ecosystems are home to a number of indigenous species of animals, such as the aquatic sitatunga, marsh mongooses and genet. There are also a few introduced animals, which include chimpanzees, roan antelope and even elephants. Plans to turn it into a sanctuary for black rhinos have so far been unsuccessful. It boasts an impressive variety of birds, some brilliantly varied butterflies, and among its array of beautiful plants are ground and tree orchids, fireball lilies which flower during the short rains, and the red coral tree which blossoms for most of the year.

Below: *The prominent but precarious Bismark's Rock in Mwanza harbour.*

Left: *To many, Lake Victoria is an inland sea, and substantial ferries such as this one docked at Mwanza are used for inter-lake connections.*

Bukoba *

The overlap between East and West Africa is a distinguishing characteristic of the whole West Lake Province, and a pleasant way of appreciating it is to sail from Mwanza to Bukoba, the western province's major town, on one of the Lake ferries. The Kagera region lies between the lake and those ill-fated countries Rwanda and Burundi, with Uganda to the north. It is considered, by some, to be the most attractive part of Tanzania.

Bukoba itself is situated on the lower slopes of the low green hills which overlook the lake. It is rarely visited by tourists, yet has an attractive location and restful atmosphere. It has two hotels, neither of which will figure in the world's top 10, though both have a rather ramshackle charm.

The people of Bukoba and of Kagera Region in general are **Haya**. Mostly Ugandan in origin, they are said to take quick advantage of formal education, though most of them are farmers, growing Robusta coffee, maize, beans, sweet potatoes and bananas. Like the Chagga, they have adopted the banana as their staple diet – they often eat them roasted, and served on banana leaves, accompanied by banana wine, which they sip through straws of grass.

Despite its remoteness, Bukoba has seen its share of action, having been defended by the Germans in World War I, and inaccurately bombed during Idi Amin's ill-fated incursions into Tanzania during the late 1970s.

BUKOBA'S BIRD LIFE

Bukoba's westerly position is reflected in some of the bird species found there and in the adjacent region. Exciting species include:
- **Grey parrot:** the familiar talking parrot..
- **Ross's turaco**.
- **Eastern grey plantain eater:** which, of course, lives on bananas.
- **Northern brown-throated weaver:** often seen in the garden of the Lake Hotel.
- Anyone walking by the lakeside might be also be rewarded by the sight of **spotted-necked otters**, which will sometimes fish and frolic close to the shore in the clear blue waters of the lake.

STANLEY AND LIVINGSTONE

After two decades of deter-mined exploring deep into Africa, David Livingstone was a well-known figure through-out the English-speaking world. Some deserters from his 1866 expedition past Lake Nyasa spread a rumour that he was dead, precipitating a search not resolved until Stanley, working for the *New York Times*, presumed to meet him under a mango tree in Ujiji. Stanley, who had dressed for the occasion and was very nervous (he half expected a hostile reception), was later asked if he had actually uttered the famous phrase. 'Yes', he replied, 'I couldn't think what else to say.' The two got on well, explored regions of Lake Tanganyika together, and were said to have wept when they parted months later.

Below: *The Mahale moun-tains, home of chimpanzees, rising from the shores of Lake Tanganyika.*

LAKE TANGANYIKA

Lake Tanganyika is one of the most interesting lakes in the world. The combination of antiquity (the dead 'fossil water' of its profound depths may be 20 million years old) and its isolation have produced many unique life forms. Most of the 250 species of fish which inhabit its rich upper waters are endemic, as are seven species of crab, and a whole range of gastropods, molluscs and crustaceans. It even has a unique water snake, the Eastern aquatic cobra, which fishes by day and sleeps on the rocks by night.

Ujiji ★

If the waters of Tanganyika are filled with fascination, its shores are no less so. The topography to the east is largely monotonous, though **Henry Morton Stanley** 'regarded the alluring face of the land with a fatuous love'. Ujiji was the spot where Stanley finally caught up with **David Livingstone**, asking his famous question under a mango tree which is today marked with a rather less attractive memorial. Ujiji's more general past, as an important terminus of the caravan route from the coast, is evident in the Arabic influences of Swahili-style houses, some with carved doors, and in a predominantly Muslim population. The town is quite large and spaciously laid out, and the shallow creek which passes for its harbour is picturesque, with flat-bottomed boats and canoes tied up in a jumble among the reeds and water lilies.

Kigoma *

Ujiji's importance declined with the ending of the slave and ivory trade, and it is now a satellite of Kigoma, 10km (6 miles) to the north. Kigoma came into prominence for the same reason as Ujiji – as the terminus of a trade route from the coast – although in Kigoma's case communications are by rail and the passengers leaving for the coast are not slaves. The **railway** was completed by the Germans in 1914, and soon afterwards appropriated by the British. For those who like to travel in style, it is not the best way to get to Kigoma, as the trip from Dar takes two days and is not the last word in comfort. But it beats walking all the way, as the explorers did.

Kigoma, like Ujiji, is a quiet town, its principle street sloping up from the interesting old station between mangoes and frangipani. The main attraction is its **waterfront,** especially when the ferry *M.V. Liemba* is in port.

Mahale Mountains National Park **

One of the destinations of the *Liemba* is **Magambo**, about 115km (70 miles) south of Kigoma. Passengers travel from the ferry to the shore by small boat, from which another boat then takes them to **Kasongo**, the headquarters of Mahale Mountains National Park. The complete trip from Kigoma takes about nine hours, and must be well planned and co-ordinated. Would-be visitors are advised to go through a reputable travel firm, or to double-check their arrangements through the National Parks Headquarters in Arusha, and the Mahale Mountains Research Office in Kigoma. There is one small, luxury camp in Mahale, but generally visitors will have to be self-sufficient.

However, travellers should not be put off by these considerations. Mahale Mountains is a delightful sanctuary, its centre-piece being a 2460m (8071ft) mountain, draped in rain-forest and inhabited by chimpanzees and other primates, with lower orders of the animal world, including birds and insects, being well represented.

M.V. LIEMBA

Kigoma's most famous boat is an old lady with an interesting past: assembled from pre-fabricated sections at the start of World War I, she was fitted out with a 4.1 gun taken from the sunken battle-cruiser *Koenigsberg* and made ready for action. When the action came, however, the *Graf von Goetzen* (as she was then known) was sent to the bottom by a Belgian bomb. The British salvaged her in 1924, and after an extensive refit she was pressed back in service. She is still going strong, ferrying passengers to different parts of Lake Tanganyika.

IS THIS A DAGAA I SEE BEFORE ME?

On moonless nights, while Lake Tanganyika's amazing aquatic cobra catches up on its sleep on the rocks by the shore, local fishermen of the Ha tribe sail out in little boats in search of shoals of *dagaa*, the small, sardine-like fish which, after being sun-dried, provides a cheap and essential protein for the lakeside people, and for many other people throughout Tanzania (they can often be seen in markets far from the Lakes). The *dagaa* are attracted to lights suspended from the boats, then panicked into stillness by a sudden beating of drums, before being hoisted up into scoop nets.

Gombe Stream National Park ★★★

Most tourists who get as far as Kigoma, however, will choose to head for the similarly beautiful, much smaller but much closer national park, Gombe Stream. Gombe is only 25km (15 miles) north of Kigoma, though access to it is again by boat. Water taxis operate out of Kigoma, taking four to six hours. Speedboats, if they can be hired, take less than an hour.

Gombe is famous for its chimpanzees, though like Mahale it contains many other species of animals. Its chimpanzees have been studied for decades by many biologists, students and rangers, but none (not even the chimpanzees) are quite as famous as the lady responsible for their world-wide reputation, however much the self-effacing **Dr Jane Goodall** would disagree. She has been connected with Gombe since 1960, and much of the credit for the studies there, and for the well-being of chimpanzees around the world, both wild and captive, must go to her. Gombe has a small guesthouse, but basically visitors have to be self-sufficient. Some camping is possible by the shore.

Left: *The flame of the Independence Monument adds warmth to the cool mountain air of Mbeya.* **Opposite:** *A chimpanzee, a primate found in both Mahale Mountains and Gombe Stream national parks on the shores of Lake Tanganyika.*

Katavi Plains National Park ★

About half way between Kigoma and Mbeya, to the southeast of Mahale Mountains, is the Katavi Plains National Park. It is about two days' drive along dirt roads from either centre – not a journey to be undertaken lightly – but within its miombo woodland and long-grass plains there is an impressive list of game and birdlife.

THE SOUTHWEST
Mbeya ★

Travellers who find themselves in Mbeya – 900km (550 miles) southwest of Dar, will be tempted to stay there, at least for a while. The town itself is small, and has little to offer tourists but relative peace and quiet and the friendliness of its people. It is Mbeya's location, among lovely mountain ranges, and its correspondingly cool climate, which endear it to expatriates and travellers. It is sometimes called the 'Scotland of Africa', and there are a number of very pleasant walks in the hills. Visitors driving into Tanzania from southern Africa through Malawi and Zambia will have to pass through Mbeya, and it is worth considering as a stop-over.

RELATIVES IN THE RAINFOREST

Remains of a hominid which lived four million years ago, recently discovered in Ethiopia, seem to confirm that our closest living relatives are the chimpanzees. Research at Gombe Stream, over rather fewer years, conforms to the same pattern. Chimpanzees have almost 100% compatibility with human DNA, a brain similar to that of man, and aspects of their behaviour are often compared to ours. Their relationships are close and complex, they hug, kiss and scream when excited or pleased, and become morbid or irritable when sad or thwarted. They sometimes use simple tools, hunt and kill monkeys, indulge in cannibalism and go to war, yet they remain fascinating and often loveable creatures.

Lake Malawi *

Last and smallest of Tanzania's Great Lakes is Malawi, sometimes known as Lake Nyasa. It is too far from the main tourist haunts to be regarded as a popular destination, but travellers to or from the south, who have the time to drive the extra 130km (80 miles) from Mbeya to the small port of **Itungi**, might be glad they have made the journey. Like Lake Tanganyika, Malawi is exceptionally rich in endemic species of fish and other water creatures. The scenery, with the **Livingstone Mountains** rising high above the head of the lake, is quite splendid, especially when seen from a boat.

Above: *A fisherman's canoe beached on the shores of beautiful Lake Malawi.*
Left: *Lake Malawi fishermen mending their nets by the shores of the great lake.*

The Lakes at a Glance

BEST TIMES TO VISIT

The period of the Long Rains and sometimes the Short Rains can be a bit dismal, whereas the months from **mid-May** to **mid-October** are usually relatively dry and comfortable.

GETTING THERE

The Lakes are not yet a popular tourist destination, but several Tanzania-based companies, such as Cordial Tours, Monason Ltd and Scan-Tan are beginning to recognize the possibilities and are offering **package tours** to places such as Gombe Stream or Mahale Mountains national parks. Alternatives for independent travellers include: Air Tanzania has regular **flights** to Mwanza and Kigoma from Dar es Salaam and Kilimanjaro airports. For tourists visiting the Serengeti **by road**, there is a reasonably straightforward route through the western corridor of the park to Mwanza. Otherwise journeys by road are long and tiresome. Both Mwanza and Kigoma are served by the central **railway** from Dar es Salaam, but it is a long and uncomfortable two day journey.

GETTING AROUND

All the lake ports are relatively small and it is possible to **walk** around the main parts of the town quite easily.
There are a few **taxis** in Mwanza and Kigoma.

Otherwise independent travel is by **car** or, where appropriate, the **ferries** or other **boats** which ply different routes on the lakes.

WHERE TO STAY

There is at present no hotel of genuine tourist standard in the Lakes region, though things are now changing rapidly as tourism is promoted and encouraged.

Lake Victoria:
Mwanza
Tilapia Hotel, tel: (068) 41067. Currently the best in Mwanza. Recently built, comfortable and with good views.
New Mwanza, tel: (068) 40620. No longer new, but reasonable and central.

Lake Tanganyika:
Kigoma
The Railway, tel: 900 and ask for Kigoma 64. Excellent situation overlooking lake.
Aqua Lodge. Recently built, Kigoma's best at present.

In *Ujiji*, just south of Kigoma, is the **Kudra Hotel**, and in *Bukoba* there is the **Lake**, an attractive colonial hotel which has seen better days.

ACCOMMODATION IN PARKS

There is a small, very exclusive lodge in Mahale Mountains National Park, and a very basic guesthouse. Gombe Stream also has a small rest-house, and there are two simple *bandas* (huts) on Rubondo Island. Travellers to any of these places must be almost entirely self-sufficient.

WHERE TO EAT

The Indian Moghlai food at the **Deluxe Hotel** in Mwanza is quite good, and the **Rex Hotel**, and **Kunaris** and **Furaha Restaurants** are good value for money.

TOURS AND EXCURSIONS

Apart from the area's national parks (and the Serengeti, reached from Mwanza) there is little to distract the traveller from the sleepy lake ports. **Saa Nane Island**, close to Mwanza, and the **Sukuma Museum** east of Mwanza, might be considered.

USEFUL CONTACTS

Mwanza code: 068.
Bukoba code: 066.
Tanzania Tourist Board, Dar es Salaam: tel: (051) 28182/27672/3, 26680.

LAKE VICTORIA	J	F	M	A	M	J	J	A	S	O	N	D
AVERAGE TEMP. °F	70	70	70	70	70	70	68	70	70	70	70	70
AVERAGE TEMP. °C	21	21	21	21	21	21	21	21	21	21	21	21
HOURS OF SUN DAILY	6	6	6	6	6	6	7	7	6	6	5	6
RAINFALL ins.	6	7	10	15	13	3	2	3	4	5	7	8
RAINFALL mm	151	168	250	370	320	85	49	76	104	138	185	193
DAYS OF RAINFALL	13	13	18	22	18	7	5	8	11	15	18	16

6
The South

Formerly known as 'The hell run', the **Tanzam Highway** from Dar es Salaam to Zambia passes through some of the most beautiful scenery in Tanzania. The road has been resurfaced over much of its length, and the journey along it is now much less harrowing (as the explorers who trudged this route 130 years ago would no doubt agree).

By-passing the lovely **Uluguru Mountains** and the little town of **Morogoro**, the highway passes through **Mikumi National Park**, and to the north of the huge **Selous Game Reserve**, before winding into the **Rubeho Mountains** and crossing the central plateau. It skirts the steep ridge on which the southern highland town of **Iringa** is perched, and from where yet another magnificent game sanctuary, **Ruaha**, is easily reached. The road then rolls on towards **Mbeya** and the Zambian border.

Other than those travelling to or from Malawi and Zambia, few tourists travel down this highway, and yet much of the country through which it passes is as wild and as wonderful as anything in Africa.

THE MOROGORO REGION

The country between Dar es Salaam and Morogoro is unremarkable for the first 160km (100 miles). At about this point the **Uluguru Mountains** become visible, lending grandeur to an already improving landscape. The mountains, rising to 2646m (8679ft), form part of the Eastern Arc, a broken series of ancient crystalline ranges

---

CLIMATE

Generally the area follows the typical climatic patterns of the East African plateau. Days are hot while nights and mornings can be pleasantly cool (especially during the dry season). The greatest threat to travel in the southern game sanctuaries is continual heavy rain. This is most likely from mid-March to mid-May, and to a lesser extent from mid-October to December. At these times certain tracks become impassable and certain airstrips inaccessible.

Opposite: *The Ruaha River and the scenic Ruaha National Park, near Msembe.*

DON'T MISS

*** **Selous Game Reserve:**
wild and immense scenery.
Offers Rufiji river trips
and foot safaris.
*** **Ruaha National Park:**
another huge and beautiful
wilderness. Noted for huge
elephants and game drives
along the Ruaha River.
** **Mikumi National Park:**
only three-and-a-half hours
drive from Dar es Salaam.
Lion, elephant, wild
dog and leopard.
** **Mufundi Tea Estates:**
relaxing cool and green
sanctuary, with golf course,
tennis and squash.
* **Udzungwa National
Park:** among mountains
and rich in endemic species.
* **Iringa:** quiet but
dramatically set capital
of the Southern Highlands.

Above: *A baobab at sunset
by the Ruaha River, home
to crocodile, hippo and
many waterbirds.*

which curves up from south-central Tanzania, reaching
almost to Kilimanjaro. On the ridges are the attractive
hamlets of the Luguru people, small clusters of thatched
huts often perched at the very end of the high spurs.

Morogoro *

Beneath the northerly slopes of the Ulugurus snuggles
the town of Morogoro. Its attractiveness owes much to
the mountains, as the charm it had in German times and
for some time afterwards has largely gone to seed.
However, it has a lively **market**, a pleasant little rock
garden and a reasonable hotel. It was once a centre for
sisal growing, but industry has declined. There is,

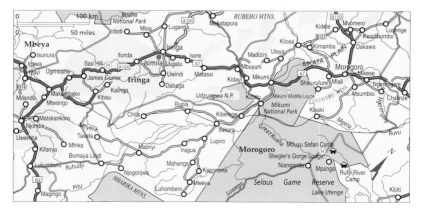

however, a flourishing **agricultural college** just outside the town, and a variety of vegetables are grown on the nearby farms. Much of this produce goes to market in Dar es Salaam. Wheat, millet, sugar cane and tobacco are among the area's other crops.

The town was the scene of fierce fighting during World War I, when the German forces, attacked by the British, put up stern resistance before blowing up their own ammunition dump and beating a strategic retreat through the Ulugurus.

Mikumi National Park **

About 80km (50 miles) southwest of Morogoro, the highway bisects Mikumi National Park. It is the third largest national park in Tanzania, a fact which surprises many visitors, as the area they frequent is relatively small, encompassing the flood plains of the unimposing but significant **Mkata River**, which flows through the park from south to north.

Surrounded on three sides by attractive mountains and hills, the park has a quiet but compelling beauty. During and just after the rains the flood plain can be as green as an Irish meadow, though the autumnal colours of the miombo woodland seen towards the end of the dry season on the slopes of the hills are deceptive – the leaves are not dying but coming to life, in anticipation of the rains.

> **MONEY GROWING ON TREES**
>
> • **Sisal** is a species of agave, introduced to the old German East Africa from Mexico. Hairy white string, rope and mats are made from the fibrous leaves, and at one time the industry was a money-spinner. These days labour-intensive plantations and the use of synthetic fibres have reduced demand.
> • Handicrafts displayed on the stumps of trees alongside the main road at the village of Mangae, between Morogoro and Mikumi National Park, are woven by women from the fronds of the young **hyphaene palm**. Anyone purchasing mats or baskets is indirectly helping Mikumi, as the villagers begin to see the value, to themselves as well as their country, of tourism.

Below: *The rustic simplicity of Mikumi Wildlife Camp, in the under-rated Mikumi National Park.*

PACHYDERM OF THE PLANT WORLD

African legend has it that God planted the spongy-barked baobab upside down, as its branches look like roots. Another story says that anyone rash enough to pluck one of the baobab's beautiful white flowers will soon afterwards be devoured by a lion (the flowers smell of carrion, and are said to be pollinated by bats and inhabited by malevolent spirits). And as if that wasn't enough, the roasted seeds of the baobab are believed to make a man attractive – not to women – but to crocodiles. The life-span of man means little to the tree itself – baobabs with a diameter of 8m (11ft) may well be over 3000 years old.

Below: *A noisy redbilled hornbill, commonly found across the southern region.*

The variety of the vegetation is matched by the diversity of animals. Mikumi has a good many elephants (most of them small, as elephants go), and it is one of the best places in Africa in which to seek the endangered wild dog and elusive leopard. Lion are commonly seen, as are giraffe, buffalo, zebra, buck, hippo and warthog. Colourful birds such as the lilac-breasted roller, and the violet-backed starling, as well as hornbill and storks, can be seen.

The light in the park is often superb, and this, together with the park's natural beauty, make it a wonderful venue for wildlife photographers.

Udzungwa National Park ★

The Tanzam highway leaves the western boundary of Mikumi by Mikumi Village. From here, a three-hour drive along a dirt track to the south takes travellers alongside the picturesque Udzungwa mountains and to the entrance of the equally picturesque national park of the same name. Gazetted in 1992, the sanctuary enjoys a growing international reputation due to its rare endemic plants and animals. Game viewing and bird watching can be enormously rewarding, but neither are easy and visitors should be prepared for some stiff

walking and scrambling. Among recent exciting discoveries are the Sanje crested mangabey (a monkey) and a previously unknown francolin, very similar to the hill partridge of the Chinese Himalaya. Self-contained accommodation is available near the park gate, and there are three beautifully sited camp sites within the park boundaries. However, campers must be entirely self-sufficient.

The Ruaha Gorge *

Beyond Mikumi village the Tanzam highway climbs up through the Rubeho Mountains, before descending to follow the course of the Ruaha River, affording, at one point, fine views down the Ruaha Gorge.

The gorge is a lonely but hauntingly attractive place, its rock-strewn river commanded by steep slopes to the south and more gradual slopes to the north, all covered by an astonishing array of **baobabs**. In the dry season, and in sharp light, their bulbous trunks and angular filigree of branches shine with a silver-whiteness, enhancing their reputation, among many Africans, as trees inhabited by ghosts.

IRINGA

Beyond this world of spirits, and beyond the final mountain passes, lies the plateau country around Iringa, capital of the Southern Highlands. Its situation atop a steep-sided ridge was strategic, as the Germans (who were largely responsible for the town's development) were well aware.

The people of the area, the **Hehe**, helped to stem the southerly expansion of the Maasai in the 19th century, and in 1889, under their formidable chief **Mkwawa**, ambushed a German-led military column as it approached from Morogoro. Using spears and other simple weapons the Hehe slaughtered almost half the German contingent, capturing guns and ammunition. Five years later Mkwawa's unfinished fort at Kalenga, 32km (20 miles) down the Ruaha track from Iringa, was attacked and the Hehe routed.

Iringa's grisly history is implicit in the names of two hills which overlook the town. One, Lundamatwe, means 'Collection of Skulls', the other, Tagamenda, 'Throw Cloths'. The slopes of the former were once festooned with the severed heads of enemy warriors, those of the latter with the clothes of the Hehe dead.

The Germans were forced out of their own highland fortress by the British during World War I, but Iringa still has the air of a dilapidated Bavarian market town.

DEATH OF MKWAWA, CHIEF OF THE HEHE

Chief Mkwawa was a renowned soldier, and it is believed that the name of his tribe came from his battle cry, a blood-curdling 'hee-hee'. After the German-led attack upon his fort at Kalenga in 1894, he fled, fighting a guerilla warfare from the hills. The Germans put a price on his head but it was only four years later, in 1898, that the same head was shattered by a bullet. Mkwawa, cornered, shot himself rather than face the inevitable hangman. His opponents, for reasons best known to themselves, had the head hacked off and shipped to Germany. In 1954 the much-travelled skull returned to Kalenga, courtesy of the German government, and is now on display in the small museum there.

SAUCY HOT-SPOT OF THE SOUTH

If Iringa's wonderful array of vegetables are eventually boiled to death in distant hotels, tourists need only grumble about the culinary legacy of the British, and reach for the Dabaga sauce. This chilli sauce is produced in Dabaga, a market-garden area some 30km (20 miles) southeast of Iringa Town. Among Tanzanians, whether at home or far overseas, Dabaga almost has a cult following. It might not turn a bland meal into cordon-bleu, but it is capable of putting life (and fire) into last week's lettuce or today's boiled beef. On a camping safari, it is worth its weight in gold.

Traces of its old beauty are still apparent, with its lovely jacarandas, its avenues of eucalyptus and pine, and the occasional show of exotic flowers. It even has a Railway Hotel, a rather odd thing to find at the top of a 200 foot-high escarpment and 80km (50 miles) from the nearest railway.

Isimila *

About 23km (14 miles) west of Iringa is one of the most important archeological sites in Africa, Isimila. Stone tools, such as hand-axes, cleavers and hammers, used some 60,000 years ago by people of the Acheulean Age, have been found in abundance, together with the bones of elephants, antelopes and pigs. Some of the bones bear the slash-marks of butchery, and some belonged to creatures now extinct, including ancient evolutionary off-shoots of the giraffe and hippo lines (the ancient hippo, *gorgops*, had eyes on stalks, a little like a crab). Not far from the site are some arresting rock stacks rising to a height of 15m (50ft).

Ruaha National Park ***

Ruaha is one of the premier wildlife parks in Africa, and, with an area of 13,000 km^2 (5000 sq miles), is only slightly smaller than the Serengeti. Its headquarters, at **Msembe,** is 130km (80 miles) west of Iringa, along what is, apart from the last sector, an excellent dirt track, which passes a series of the Hehe's traditional mud and wattle thatched huts.

Right: *Stone Age tools from the important site at Isimila, near Iringa.* **Opposite:** *Tea pickers performing their highly selective task on the estates at Mufindi in the attractive Southern Highlands.*

The famous East African ornithologist John Williams once said of Ruaha that 'of all the East African faunal preserves it is the park of the future'. 20 years on, his prophecy awaits its inevitable fulfilment, for this glorious wilderness remains largely undeveloped and undiscovered.

The **Ruaha River** and its tributaries (some of them 'sand rivers' for much of the year) are the focal points for most visitors, as they are for many animals. Along these watercourses grow wild figs, tamarinds, palms and the lovely winterthorn trees *Acacia albida*, all of which provide food and shade for the animals, and which give greener definition to the often dry, always magnificent landscapes.

Parts of the land are dominated by baobabs, though in general the country is covered by *Combretum* and *Commiphora* woodland, with a scattering of acacia. Here and there, throughout the rest of the park, are open areas of black-cotton grassland, where ostriches, Grant's gazelle and sometimes lion and cheetah might be found.

Mufindi Tea Estates ★★

A wonderful complement to a safari in Ruaha is a visit to the Mufindi Tea Estates, which are about 100km (60 miles) southwest of Iringa. After the rigours of the bush, the green luxuriance and cool climate of Mufindi, where log fires burn in the dry season evenings, is a rest-cure for body and soul.

RUAHA SAFARI

Some of the highlights are:
• **Elephant:** Ruaha is renowned for its huge bull elephants, though many were slaughtered in the 1980s by poachers. Family groups are often seen bathing or crossing the river close to the Park HQ at Msembe. Calves will hang onto their mother's tail with their trunks as they step into the water, or, if completely submerged, will use their trunks as periscopes.
• **Roan antelope:** a small herd is resident in the wooded hill country close to Msembe.
• **Greater kudu:** sometimes seen along the river drive.
• **Crocodile** and **hippo:** found in various reaches of the river, including the so-called 'Hippo Pool' close to the bridge which takes visitors into the park.
• **Birdlife:** seen throughout the Park, though the river drive is one of the best areas. Species include the African skimmer, Von der Decken's and red-billed hornbills, and the rare Eleonora's falcon (a passage migrant).

BOEHM'S BEE-EATER

Eight members of the beautiful bee-eater family might
be seen in The Selous. One
of them, Boehm's Bee-eater,
is quite uncommon, but
might be easily observed
and photographed in the
Rufiji River Camp, where it
nests. The nest is little more
than a tunnel in the ground,
sometimes astonishing close
to a well-used footpath.
Patrons of the camp can be
quite alarmed when a slender,
bottle-green missile comes
hurtling from its underground
'silo' to perch on a nearby
branch, awaiting the next
unfortunate bee (which the
birds devenom by holding
them in their bill and rubbing
them against a branch).

The estates themselves are interesting, with a pleasing geometric beauty. Guided tours around the processing factory can be arranged, but it is the adjacent golf course, a heavenly green after the scorched fairways of the coast, the rich forests and fishing lakes, as well as the homely food and hospitality at the little clubhouse, which attract most visitors.

SELOUS GAME RESERVE

The Selous (pronounced 'Sell-oo') is the oldest and biggest game reserve in Africa and among the wildest sanctuaries on earth. It extends over more than 50,000km^2 (19,300 sq miles) of miombo woodland, terminalia thicket, open grassland and gallery forest, watered by the **Rufiji River**, its network of tributaries, and its ox-bow lakes. Few travellers venture into the almost trackless wastes south of the Rufiji, and those who do must be entirely self-sufficient. The reserve's northern sector is the only area in any way developed for tourism, but even this is huge and wild, although its topography is given scale by hills, the adjacent Uluguru mountains, and the Rufiji itself.

Right: *The Rufiji River, which waters the huge wilderness of the Selous Game Reserve.*
Opposite: *Boat safari helmsmen and game scouts on Lake Tagala in Selous Game Reserve.*

Northern Selous: Eastern sector

The drive to the Selous from Dar es Salaam, southwards along 130km (80 miles) of pot-holed tarmac to Kibiti, and 105km (66 miles) of dirt track beyond that, can be long and tiring. The area which most visitors first see is the country around the **Rufiji River Camp**, just across the reserve's northeastern boundary.

The tented camp stands on low sandy cliffs overlooking the river from which it takes its name, and is situated among a lovely, isolated grove of woodland rich in birdlife. It is the river which captures the imagination, and a boat safari, through pods of wallowing hippo and past basking crocodiles, is the highlight of the visit for most people. Buffalo, waterbuck, and impala can usually be seen in the water meadows. Giraffes have not yet found their way across the Rufiji, but might be seen on the northern banks, while elephant and lion are always possibilities. Water birds are plentiful, and include the African skimmer, kingfishers, goliath heron and the rarely seen Pel's fishing owl.

In places the river banks are lined by avenues of headless borassus palms, their stately, spindle-shaped boles standing like regiments of giant aliens. Against a Selous sunset, with the river glittering with golden fragments of light and the Uluguru Mountains blue-grey in the distance, the palms make a fantastic sight.

RUGBY MEN

It was an English ex-public schoolboy by the name of **Ionides** who was responsible for expanding the Selous to its present vastness. Nellie Grant, mother of the writer Elspeth Huxley, met him in 1959 and reported that 'he is a bit round the bend' (he was known to scorn underclothes, allow himself to be bitten by venomous snakes and eat hornbills). He is buried at the foot of Nandanga Mountain. Also buried in the reserve, and also a product of Rugby School in England, was **Frederick Courtney Selous**, a white hunter for Theodore Roosevelt and a leader of the famous scouts who were sent by Cecil Rhodes to capture land in what became Rhodesia (now Zimbabwe). Selous was also slightly eccentric, with the habit of hunting lions from horseback minus his trousers; his grave is close to the spot, near the Beho-Beho river, where he was shot by a sniper's bullets in the midst of a skirmish during World War I.

WHISTLING THORN

The whistling thorn (*Acacia drepanolobium*) is covered in natural galls, or lesions, and, like all acacias, by sharp thorns. It gets its name from the sound made by the wind as it passes over the tiny holes in the hollow galls, and from the vibration the wind causes in the slender thorns. The galls are inhabited by creatures such as cremogaster ants, which gain some protection from the acacia's thorns, and which, in turn, are thought to deter some animals from browsing on the foliage. When the foliage dies off, the intricate mass of silver-grey galls and spiky branches has a fierce and abstract beauty.

From their bare tops, here and there along the river, fish eagles, perched like alert sentinels, throw back their snow-white heads and send their evocative call echoing along the waterway.

The bush around the camp is almost as interesting, with mature miombo woodland close by, reminding northern visitors of the broad-leaved woodlands of home, and less familiar tracts of whistling thorn beyond. Wild dogs, elephants and other animals might sometimes be seen in the shady miombo, with giraffes, greater kudu, eland, zebra and wildebeest often among the whistling thorn. In the dry season they file through the acacias to drink at the river, or its associated lakes.

Northern Selous: East-central sector

A leisurely one-and-a-half hour's drive or so from Rufiji River brings the traveller to the centre of a delightful area of *Terminalia spinasa* parkland and waterside terraces which, after the rains, are beautifully lush and green. Plentiful water and grazing attract a variety of game, and lions are common, though (as always in the southern parks) the wildlife enthusiast or photographer has to work hard for his or her pleasures. Two camps, **Mbuyu** and **Mbuyuni** (named after baobab trees) serve this area. They are both on the Rufiji.

Right: *One of the Rufiji River's many hippos takes to the water after a night's grazing on the banks.*

Left: *Endangered because of their susceptibility to diseases borne by domesticated canines, sightings of wild dog have become a highlight of safaris in the southern national parks.*

Northern Selous: Beho-Beho sector

West of the Mbuyu/Mbuyuni area the *Terminalia* woodland degenerates into scrub as the land rises towards Beho-Beho, an expanse of hilly terrain and open grassland which Dr Alan Rodgers, one of the greatest authorities on the Selous, has described as 'some of the most magnificent wildlife country in East Africa'. Many game animals, including lion, wild dogs and hordes of hyenas, seem to agree with him. Elephant are often seen in the groves of doum palm alongside watercourses or sand rivers, and sable antelope inhabit the wooded hills in the northwest.

Rhino, once common in the area, are beginning to recover from the poaching blitz of the 1980s, and hippo and crocodiles may be seen in one of Beho-Beho's main features, **Lake Tagalala**. Ospreys, palm-nut vultures and many species of water or grassland birds might be observed in the vicinity of the lake.

Other attractions in the Beho-Beho sector include the **hot springs**, a pretty picnic spot where you may bathe or swim in the warm waters, **Stiegler's Gorge** (on the Rufiji) and **Selous' grave**, close to Beho-Beho Camp. Among the old trenches overlooking the spot where Selous met his death, rifle cartridges may still be discovered. Visitors to the reserve still sometimes place

FOOT SAFARIS

In the Selous, as in other game reserves (but **not** most National Parks), visitors can experience some of the thrills of old-time safaris by walking, rather than driving, through the bush, accompanied by an armed game scout. Such safaris can be disappointing for photographers of big game, as animals will usually avoid people on foot and vanish into the vegetation. Now and again, however, lions, elephants or buffalo remain unaware of approaching humans, allowing for an exciting, though rarely dangerous, encounter. Big game or not, a foot safari allows participants a fascinating insight into life in the bush, where the spoor of a jackal, the glimpse of a wild flower, the smell of a dead antelope, or the sound of a snapping twig can arouse a whole spectrum of emotions, including wonder – and fear.

SACRED SCARABS

There are various species
of scarab beetle, or as they
are more prosaically known,
dung beetles. The scarab
was sacred to the ancient
Egyptians, who perhaps
recognized its enterprise
and industry. During or
immediately after the rains,
the beetles can often be
seen paddling balls of buffalo
or elephant dung across the
tracks, using their back pair
of legs. The female beetle,
after burying the ball of dung
in a suitable spot, lays her
eggs in it. The resulting grub
enters the world surrounded
by what (to them) is an
irresistible and seemingly
inexhaustible supply of food.

Above: *The hot springs
in the Beho-Beho area of
the northern Selous.*
Below: *Sand Rivers Lodge,
overlooking the Rufiji River,
Selous Game Reserve.*

wild flowers on the grave in sentimental but sincere
tribute, using beer bottles as vases (Selous, who was tee-
total, might not have approved).

Beho-Beho and its adjacent countryside now
encompasses a new luxury lodge, **Sand Rivers**, which
is on the Rufiji, as well as the long-established Selous
Safari Camp, situated on the slopes of a hill above
a small tributary of the Beho-Beho river. A third camp,
Stiegler's Gorge, stands close to the narrows of the
Rufiji from which it takes its name.

The South at a Glance

BEST TIMES TO VISIT

The months from **mid-May** to **mid-October** are normally dry, and relatively cool in the mornings and evenings, though days can still be hot. This dry season is the most comfortable time of year, and the best in terms of road conditions in the parks and game reserves.

GETTING THERE

Most people travel through the area by **road** along the Tanzam Highway. The road is very good, except for the initial stage from Dar which is pot-holed. The Selous can be reached on a poor road from Dar via Kibiti, from Morogoro or from Mikumi National Park.
Flights can be arranged through Coastal Travels, Precision Air or Sky Tours. All the major camps have airstrips. Visitors travelling to the Selous by **rail** can be collected at Fuga Halt by prior arrangement with the camp concerned.

GETTING AROUND

Most tourists travel in their own **car**, their **tour** company's vehicle, or in one provided by the particular park lodge. Iringa and Morogoro are small enough to **walk** around.

WHERE TO STAY

Morogoro
The Morogoro Hotel, tel: (056) 3270/1/2. Only large hotel in area, 2km (1¼ miles)

out of town. Golf course, tennis, dining room.

Mikumi National Park
Mikumi Wildlife Camp, contact the Oyster Bay Hotel, Dar es Salaam, tel: (051) 68631. Located just inside the main gate of the park. Simple and rustic.
Mikumi Wildlife Lodge, contact Savannah Tours, Dar es Salaam, tel: (051) 25752, fax: (051) 44568. Unsophisticated but friendly and informal.

Ruaha National Park
Mwagusi Camp, contact Coastal Travels. Luxury camp, imaginatively designed and well situated. The best camp in Ruaha at the moment.
Ruaha River Camp, contact Coastal Travels. Simple but very good food, fine scenery. A deservedly popular camp.

Selous Game Reserve
Beho-Beho, contact Oyster Bay Hotel. Overpriced but relatively secluded and pleasantly situated close to Selous' grave and the Hot Springs.
Mbuyu Tented Camp, contact Southern Tanganyika Game Safaris, Dar es Salaam, tel: (051) 24896, fax: (051) 24897. No longer one of the premier camps but still very pleasant and relaxed.
Mbuyuni, contact Coastal Travels. One of the best camps in the Selous – small, private and well run.

Rufiji River Camp, tel: (051) 21281, fax: (051) 75165. A simple camp beautifully located on a low headland overlooking the Rufiji.
Sand Rivers, contact Nomad Safaris, tel: (051) 46862/3, fax: (051) 46863. Exclusive lodge situated by the Rufiji River. Six luxury cottages built in rustic style with dining room (good food), swimming pool. Game drives, boat safaris and foot safaris offered.

WHERE TO EAT

Not too much choice, except in some of the lodges and camps and at **Mufindi Guest House**. The camps run by the Fox family in Ruaha (**Ruaha River Camp** and **Mwagusi Camp**) have a reputation for some very good farm-house style cooking.

TOURS AND EXCURSIONS

Game drives are offered in the parks, as part of a package or booked as an optional extra through the lodges. In the Selous, **boat trips** on the Rufiji or Lake Tagalala are available, as are **foot safaris**. Mbuyuni Camp offers boat trips down the Rufiji, through the delta to Mafia Island.

USEFUL CONTACTS

Iringa code: 064.
Mbeya code: 065.
Coastal Travels: tel: (051) 37479, fax: (051) 46045.
Precision Air: tel: (051) 30800.
Air Tanzania: tel: (051) 46643.

7
Zanzibar and Pemba

Forty kilometres (25 miles) east of Bagamoyo, off the mid-Tanzanian coast, lies the island of Unguja or, as it is more commonly known to westerners, Zanzibar. It is only 85km (53 miles) long and 20km (12 miles) wide, but for centuries its importance has been out of all proportion to its size. In the 19th century it was said that 'when the flute is played in Zanzibar, they dance at the lakes', a tribute to the far-reaching powers of the Omani Sultans who made Zanzibar the seat of their Imamate, and their home. It was the earlier sultans, particularly **Said the Great**, founder of the Zanzibar sultanate in 1832, who brought prosperity to the islands, largely by encouraging the planting of cloves, and by promoting the slave trade on which the plantations depended.

But there is much more to Unguja, and its sister island **Pemba**, away to the north, than history. They are low-lying, with no significant mountains or rivers, but they are pleasant, fertile places, their sultry air still heavy, at times, with the scent of spices.

A Brief History of Zanzibar

The early history of the islands remains obscure, although they were mentioned in *The Periplus of the Erythrean Sea*, a seafarers' guide written by a **Greek** merchant in AD 60. It is fairly certain that **Arabs** had begun to settle in Zanzibar by the 9th century, and that 400 years later **Shirazi Persians** made their home there. By 1045 the indigenous population had already adopted Islam.

CLIMATE

The climate of Zanzibar, Pemba and Mafia is typically coastal: generally hot and humid but often tempered by sea breezes. Average daytime temperatures are around 30°C (86°F). The hottest months are from November to March, but from June to October the southeast monsoon brings cooler, drier weather. From March to May the Long Rains bring some heavy showers. The Short Rains (less predictable and lighter) occur between October and December.

Opposite: *The old Arab fort and House of Wonders (behind) in Stone Town.*

DON'T MISS

*** **Stone Town:** a leisurely stroll around the old streets is what Zanzibar is all about.
** **Beaches:** on the northeast coast, the finest in Tanzania.
** **Spice Tours:** a great way to take in the full breadth of Zanzibar island and its history up-country.
** **Pemba Island:** some interesting ruins, a remoter way of life, and some good fishing, diving and snorkelling.
* **Mafia Island:** not often visited, but also good for fishing, diving and snorkelling.

Opposite: *The crumbling house of Tippu Tip, best known of Zanzibar's slave traders and a prosperous merchant.*
Below: *Graves at Zanzibar's first mosque, the 12th-century house of worship at Kizimkazi.*

Zanzibar's first mosque, at Kizimkazi, was built in 1107. The Persians and Arabs passed on commercial know-how as well as genes, inspiring vigorous trade with countries as far afield as China. This buoyant interchange was depressed by two centuries of **Portuguese** rule, beginning in 1500. But by 1700 the Portuguese were in retreat, ousted by the resurgent **Omani Arabs**.

Omani rule along the coast soon became absolute, though there were many feuds among the powerful families, and a few indigenous chiefs retained power in

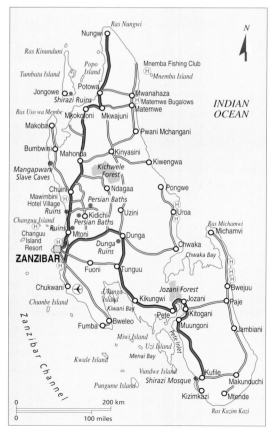

the remoter areas. But Zanzibar's rise to fame – and notoriety – really began in 1832, when **Sultan Seyid Said** (Said the Great), chose to control his extensive Imamate from Zanzibar rather than Muscat, the Omani capital on the Arabian peninsula

Capital of the Slave Trade

On the death of Said in 1856, the Omani sultanate broke away from Zanzibar. By then Zanzibar and Pemba were well on the way to prosperity, based on the dramatic expansion of the **clove** plantations, and the equally dramatic expansion of the **slave trade**.

The slave trade had existed for centuries before the sultans came to Zanzibar, but not on such a terrible and escalating scale. The British, who had established an early presence in Zanzibar, opposed the trade and, through their political agents, notably **Atkins Hamerton** and **John Kirk**, gained the confidence of the two most influential sultans of the period, Said and his son **Barghash**. The British were instrumental in limiting and finally ending the slave trade, though it was almost 50 years after the closing of the infamous Zanzibar slave market, in 1873, that slavery was completely eradicated from mainland Tanganyika.

TIPPU TIP

The best known of all Zanzibari slave traders was Tippu Tip (his real name was Hamed Bin Muhammed El Murjebi). He was ruthless and determined, but also a man of intelligence, ability and courage. On one occasion, when hit by three arrows during a skirmish, he turned on his assailants and, together with his companions, killed more than 1000 within an hour. Stanley regarded him as 'the most remarkable man I had met among the Arabs, Waswahili and the half-castes in Africa', and the slaver, with a personal retinue of 96 (including his 35 wives and concubines) sailed from Zanzibar to West Africa as part of Stanley's final expedition in 1887. Tippu Tip enjoyed retirement as a wealthy and respected gentleman, in his house in Zanzibar Town. The house still stands.

**BRITAIN'S MAN
IN ZANZIBAR**

John Kirk was, perhaps, the best-known of several very able British consuls attached to Zanzibar. A former travelling partner of Livingstone's and a friend and advisor of Sultan Barghash, his influence was enormous. He helped to end the slave trade, and also assisted various explorers (although Stanley detested him). His house at Mbweni, just south of Zanzibar town, and built for him by Barghash, may still be visited. It was here that Kirk, an expert botanist, lovingly created an experimental garden, introducing improved varieties of native food-plants and trees, and other plants likely to prove of economical value to the islands.

The Explorers

From the late 1850s to the mid 1870s, up to 30,000 slaves a year were brought to Zanzibar. Throughout the same period, a series of extraordinary men were heading in the opposite direction. **Burton** and **Speke** passed through Zanzibar in 1857, to seek the source of the Nile. In 1866 **Livingstone** set out from Zanzibar on his last journey, returning (in a coffin) in 1874. In 1872 **H.M. Stanley** sailed into Zanzibar to a hero's welcome after his historic meeting with Livingstone in Ujiji.

The explorers were often helped by the Zanzibari slave traders, who, however ruthless, regarded slaving as legitimate business, the ethics of which would seldom, if ever, have crossed their minds. The sultans, too, would have been puzzled by western moralities, not least because of American and European involvement in the West African slave trade. They signed anti-slavery legislation only under pressure, but the benefits which the sultans brought to Zanzibar should not be overlooked. Their legacy included a thriving economy, which the clove plantations easily sustained long after the decline of the slave trade, telegraph and shipping links with Europe, and in Zanzibar Town a clean water supply.

Revolution

Zanzibar became a British protectorate in 1890, and for more than 70 years enjoyed relative peace and prosperity. Apart from a brief naval action at the start of World War II, when the German battle cruiser *Koenigsberg* shelled and sank the British warship *Pegasus* in Zanzibar harbour, the islands were not directly affected by the

two world wars. As soon as the British left, however, *Pax Britannica* left on the same tide. In 1963 **Sayyid Jamshid Bin Abdulla Bin Khalif**, last of the Zanzibari sultans, came to the throne. In January 1964, one month after Zanzibar's independence, he was overthrown in a bloody revolution, during which about 13,000 people, mostly Arabs, were slaughtered in an orgy of killing. A generation later, peace has returned to the islands, which are beginning to recover some of their former autonomy and prosperity, and to attract more tourists.

Above: *The gazebo in Jamituri Gardens on Stone Town's seafront.*
Opposite: *'Livingstone's House', Zanzibar. The house was, in fact, made available to the explorer by Sultan Barghash.*

THE STONE TOWN

The Stone Town is Zanzibar's old quarter. It has been called 'the only functioning historical city in East Africa' and is so little changed since the 1850s that Burton and Speke might just, it seems, have left for the interior last week. The best way to appreciate this is to walk, as the explorers did, through the old streets.

Seafront

There are no prescribed routes for a tour of Stone Town – but perhaps the seafront is an appropriate place to start. People arriving by sea will pass the old dhow harbour as they leave the dockside complex. The great ocean-going dhows are now mostly gone, but visitors might see a few alongside the wharf, or, better still, under sail against a flaming sunset, from the seafront itself. Smaller dhows are still common.

THE FACES OF STONE TOWN

The faces of most Zanzibaris are a living documentary of the island's cosmopolitan past, while their clothes are an indication of their devotion to Islam. Traditional *kanzu*, an ankle-length robe worn by men, and *bui-bui*, the long black gown worn by women, are not as evident as they were. But the embroidered caps favoured by Muslim men are still popular, and many women still regard the world through large and beautiful dark eyes, enhanced by *kohl*, all other features screened from the gaze of men by a headscarf and the flowing *bui-bui*.

DOORWAYS TO HISTORY

Zanzibar doors have become renowned. Custom ordained that the doorway of a house should be built before the house itself, presumably to exert a benign influence over the completed building. The ritual was given added strength by Koranic scripts and representational carvings which adorn the doorways. The Zanzibar door was traditionally made of teak, and was set in a square frame, covered by delicate and slender carvings. Indian influences during the 19th century modified this prototype, producing doors with arched tops and more elaborate floral designs. Motifs to be seen on such doors include the lotus (symbol of reproductive power), the fish (fertility), the chain (security) and the frankincense tree (wealth).

A short distance from the dockyard gate Mizingani Road begins its southwesterly course along one of the most historic seafronts in the world. Near its northern end is the ornately attractive **Ismaili Dispensary**, presented to the Aga Khan's followers in Zanzibar on the occasion of Queen Victoria's Jubilee. A little further along the road, still heading southwest, is the former Sultan's Palace, now called the **People's Palace**, and open to the public. First occupied by a reigning sovereign in 1911, it previously accommodated members of the royal family and the harem. In the graveyard alongside, Said the Great and other sultans lie buried. The interior of the palace is comfortably rather than splendidly furnished, but it provides interesting insights into a vanished and exotic period of Zanzibar's history.

Adjacent to the palace is the **House of Wonders**, the *Beit el-Ajaib*, built by Sultan Barghash in 1883. Together with the original palace it was damaged by shell-fire during a scuffle for the accession in 1896, when British warships intervened, precipitating 'the shortest war in history' (it lasted for 45 minutes). The Beit el-Ajaib is presently being restored to its palatial splendour, minus the lions and other animals which were once kept caged outside its gates. It contains the most beautiful examples of 'Zanzibar doors' in East Africa.

Right: *The House of Wonders, built as a ceremonial palace in 1883 by Sultan Barghash.*

A little further down the seafront stands the **Arab Fort**, with its ochre-coloured walls. Never more than a primitive structure, it withstood an attack by the Mazrui Arabs from Mombasa in 1754, and was afterwards used as a gaol. As late as 1890 criminals sentenced to death were still publicly beheaded by the sword, just outside the walls at the back of the fort. Enclosed by a promontory to the

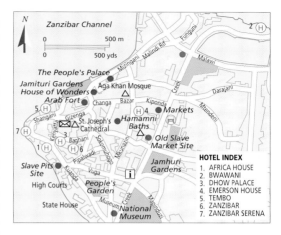

west of the fort is the district known as Shangani, 'The Place of Beads'. The original **slave market** (in the square now overlooked by the Serena Hotel) once stood here and, appropriately, the house of **Tippu Tip**, most notorious of the Zanzibar slavers, can be found nearby, in a shadowy, seldom-visited corner of the town.

A few doors away is the **Africa House Hotel**, a less ominous building with its own nostalgia. It was formerly the British Club, and clings, with stiff upper lip, to its colonial past. Its seaward-facing terrace is popular at sundown. The **Zanzibar Hotel**, in the same district, is another interesting old building, its rooms traditionally constructed from mangrove poles. The poles, impervious to termites, are still used throughout East Africa, and their export to the Gulf and elsewhere, by dhow, is one of the oldest, if declining, forms of trade in the region.

In the southern area of Stone Town is the **National Museum**. It contains various exhibits and relics pertinent to Zanzibar, including some of Livingstone's letters and his medicine chest. At the back of the museum is the oldest carved door in Stone Town. Close by on Kaunda Road are the **High Courts**, with their blend of Arabic and Portuguese architecture, and the **State House**.

FINDING YOUR WAY IN STONE TOWN

● **Walking** is undoubtedly the best (and often only) way to negotiate the fascinating narrow streets of Stone Town.
● **Guides** are not essential, but the best of them, often older, know their town and its absorbing history. Visitors should ask for a guide at their hotel or any tourist centre.
● If you choose to discover Stone Town on your own, however, you can 'lose' yourself in the maze of alleyways without too much fear of being lost for long, or of having anything **stolen**, though visitors should use a little common sense (e.g. by not wearing expensive jewellery).
● Don't take **photographs** without asking.

THE CATHEDRAL

Stone Town's Cathedral Church of Christ, built on the site of the old slave market, is an imposing building. Inside the altar was erected on the same spot as the slave whipping post had been, and a stained glass window commemorates the British sailors who died on anti-slaving patrols. On a pillar beside the chancel is a crucifix, made from the tree under which Livingstone's heart was buried. Interred behind the cathedral altar are the remains of Bishop Steere, who supervised the building of the cathedral and who, every Friday, had the Victorian cheek to preach to Muslims in the adjoining Chapel of the Blessed Sacrament. This obviously didn't upset the reigning sultan, Barghash, who donated a clock to adorn the Cathedral tower.

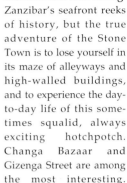

Above: *Coffee is served – thick, black and strong.*
Below: *The Cathedral Church of Christ, founded in 1873 on the slave market.*

Markets Old and Young

Zanzibar's seafront reeks of history, but the true adventure of the Stone Town is to lose yourself in its maze of alleyways and high-walled buildings, and to experience the day-to-day life of this sometimes squalid, always exciting hotchpotch. Changa Bazaar and Gizenga Street are among the most interesting. Except in the heat of early afternoon the streets bustle with unpretentious enterprise. The tiny shops are home, as well as business, to a multitude of traders and craftsmen, their goods and handiwork awaiting buyers throughout the slow-paced day. Meanwhile clocksmiths sit cross-legged on raised floors, surrounded by heaps of broken watches, tailors pedal away on sewing machines, carpenters hammer and saw, and coffee sellers weave through the crowds with their Arabic-style pots, heated on trays of smouldering charcoal.

Close to the town's main markets, just west of Creek Road, is the **Cathedral Church of Christ** which, until 1883, was the site of the infamous slave market. It is difficult now to imagine the scenes that took place here,

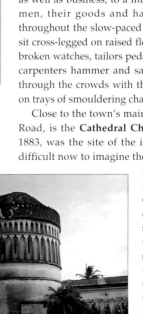

when 300 slaves or more might be herded and paraded here each day in the late afternoon. They were now subjected to the most intimate and embarrassing scrutiny. Muscles and teeth were examined, sticks were thrown for the male slaves to retrieve, and the younger, more attractive women were lasciviously fondled.

Left: *Just a few of the spices and fruits to be seen (and sampled) in Zanzibar.*

Zanzibar's Roman Catholic cathedral, **St Joseph's**, on the edge of Shângani, has a less disturbing history. There are mosques too, as one might expect in Zanzibar, the most notable being the **Aga Khan** and the **Bohora**. Hinduism is represented by the **Shakti Temple**. Other Stone Town buildings of interest include the old British Consulate (now Mackenzie Building), where several famous explorers stayed, the Hamamni Persian Baths and, on Kenyatta Road, General Mathews House (now a dental surgery).

AROUND UNGUJA ISLAND

Zanzibar's blend of troubled history and relaxing peacefulness can be experienced outside, as well as inside, the Stone Town. So-called **'Spice Tours'** introduce the visitor to the fascinating world of Zanzibar's spice-growing areas, and are usually combined with a mobile history lesson. Tourists will catch interesting glimpses of life among the villages, with their little mud-and-wattle houses roofed with palm thatch or corrugated iron. And on the roads they might see Indian-style ox-carts or Zanzibar's unique country buses which, with their wooden coachwork, glass-less windows and slatted seats, look more like early 19th-century railway carriages, and are just about as comfortable.

SKELETONS – BUT NOT IN THE CUPBOARDS

The custom of burying slaves alive in the walls of houses under construction is thought to have been fairly common in old Zanzibar. Skeletons were discovered in the foundations of the old Cable and Wireless building, erected on the site of the original slave market at Shangani by Sultan Barghash to bring enlightenment to Zanzibar. A more awful irony distinguishes a building called Mambo Msigee on the tip of the Shangani promontory. It was formerly occupied by such anti-slavery luminaries as the Universities Mission to Central Africa and Sir John Kirk, who were all blithely unaware that living slaves had been entombed in the walls which sheltered them.

SPICE TOURS

The **clove** is still king on Zanzibar and Pemba, but with declining markets there has been some pressure to diversify, and people taking the Spice Tour might be shown nutmeg, black pepper, cinnamon, cardamom, chilli, vanilla, peppermint and the sharply citrus-fragrant lemon grass. Also charming the senses are an array of exotic fruits – plantains and bananas, mangos, pawpaws, breadfruit, jackfruit, avocados, guavas, mulberries, durians, litchis, pomegranates, oranges, grapefruit, and limes. Spice tours can be arranged through your hotel or a tourist information centre, but shop around and agree on an itinerary and fee before setting out.

ENDANGERED MONKEY, SCARCE LEOPARD

Jozani Forest's main attraction is the Zanzibar red colobus, *Colobus badius kirkii*, a beautiful and endangered monkey endemic to the Island and named after the well-known British Consul. Other wildlife is limited but interesting, and includes Sykes monkeys, suni antelopes, bush pigs, bush babies, hyraxes and mongooses. The Zanzibar leopard, thought until recently to be extinct, is now known to be alive and well and living (albeit precariously) in the bush and scrub of the southern part of the island.

Soon after leaving the town centre, the Spice Tours will pass **Livingstone's House**, now occupied by the Zanzibar Tourist Corporation. The missionary-explorer stayed here in 1866 prior to his final expedition. A little further north is **Marahubi Palace**, built by Sultan Barghash to house his harem. He did not live to enjoy his visits there, and 11 years after his death it burned down. It is now in ruins, but ruins can be romantic, and Marahubi's melancholic wistfulness is not unpleasant. Further north still is another palace, **Mtoni**, once occupied by Said the Great and his huge household.

Less than 20km (12 miles) north of Mtoni is **Mwangapwani**. Here, by a beautiful crescent of white sand shelving into the blue ocean, lies a dark coral cave said (probably without foundation) to have been used for holding slaves after 1873, when their export from Zanzibar was forbidden. Another place of historical interest north of Zanzibar Town are the disused **Persian Baths** at Kidichi, built by Sultan Said.

In the centre of Zanzibar Island, at **Dunga**, are the ruins of a fortified palace, former home of a tyrannical local chief. Further south, near Pete, is **Jozani Forest**, a wildlife sanctuary where endemic and endangered Zanzibar red colobus monkeys may be observed. And in the extreme south, some 30km (20 miles) beyond Jozani, the traveller will find traces of an old Shirazian settlement by the seashore at **Kizimkazi**. Its mosque was the first to be built on the East African coast (in 1107).

Left: *Clear, warm waters, for so many one of the attractions of Zanzibar, at Mangapwani, north of Stone Town.*
Opposite: *Tourists stop off at Marahubi to see the atmospheric ruins of Sultan Barghash's harem.*

Sea and Shore

Too much history can be as cloying as the fragrance of cloves, and a convenient complement to the past is a day or two in the present, and by the sea. Zanzibar's **beaches**, particularly along its eastern seaboard ('The Sunrise Coast') are beautiful and unspoilt, idyllic locations for lotus-eating laziness. The villagers along this coast are mostly involved in fishing, though other occupations include cattle raising, mat-making, lime-burning and the making of embroidered Muslim caps.

Another relaxing possibility is to take a boat trip to one of Zanzibar's offshore islets. The most popular of these is commonly known as **Prison** (*Changuu*) Island. Another islet with a sombre name is **Grave** (*Chapwani*) Island. Its name relates to the cemetery there, designated by Sultan Barghash as a graveyard for British sailors killed on anti-slavery patrols, though some graves go back to the early decades of the 19th century. Despite their names, the islands are far from grim, and are known for their beaches, swimming, snorkelling and sunbathing.

PEMBA

Nearly 50km (32 miles) to the north is an island not much smaller than Unguja itself. Pemba, known to the Arabs as *Al Khudra*, the Green Island, is little visited by tourists, although it is now beginning to realise its potential.

PRISON ISLAND

Originally owned by an Arab who detained unruly slaves on it, Prison Island was later bought by Lloyd Mathews, who had a prison built there in 1893. The ruins of the prison (it was never used) still stand, but despite its name the small island is an attractive place, with fine beaches, pleasant woodland walks and a small restaurant. The woodland is inhabited by tiny suni antelopes, as well as a variety of birds – including introduced peafowl. The animal which arouses most interest, however, is the giant land tortoise, originally from Aldabra. There are about 50 of these huge reptiles, which hiss like snakes when threatened but which are harmless.

Right: *Drying cloves on Pemba Island, the real 'Isle of Cloves'.*

Cloves

Like Unguja, Pemba's 19th-century history was dominated by cloves and slaves. Pemba is, in fact, the true island of cloves, and although the industry is declining and prices falling, much of Pemba is still covered by clove trees, some of them a century and a half old. During the harvest season, between July and December, the oily fragrance of cloves drifts over the island in an aromatic mist. Pickers climb the trees, which can attain a height of 15m (50ft), by means of ropes or ladders, snapping off clusters of unopened buds, greenish or yellowish-red in colour. These are collected in baskets and laid out in the sun for four to seven days, until their colour deepens into the familiar dark brown, when they are graded and packed for export. They are eventually, of course, used in cooking and baking, but also in the manufacture of aromatic and medicinal oils, and in Indonesia, to flavour cigarettes.

Around the Island

The many ruins around the island bear testimony to the its older, more general past. At **Chake Chake**, Pemba's principal town, there are remains of a 13th-century Shirazi settlement, a mosque which is said to be one of the finest

---

EL TOREADORES

The Portuguese left little evidence of their stay in Pemba, with one unlikely exception, the bull fight, held in the hot months of December, January and February. As in the Portuguese version of the sport the animals are not killed, nor do they bear much resemblance to the morose and massive fighting bulls of Andalusia. They are of hump-backed *zebu* stock and according to one aficionado enter the ring (an open space among the mangoes) wearing, on their faces, 'a benign, cow-like expression'.

of its type on the coast of East Africa, and a Muslim fort (now converted into a hospital). At **Pujini**, 11km (7 miles) north of Chake Chake, there is a 14th-century fortified settlement, and at **Ras Mkumbuu**, an attractive headland on the western coast, the ruins of an Islamic settlement established in the 9th or even 8th century.

The island has various wild animals, not least among which is the Pemba puddle frog, and an endemic fruit bat, the Pemba flying fox. But wildlife enthusiasts who seek a superabundance of beautiful creatures must go down to the sea, and beneath it. And for those who prefer less demanding pastimes, Pemba has many marvellous and virtually unknown beaches.

Mafia Island *

Situated 160km (100 miles) south of Zanzibar Island, Mafia is 394km^2 (152 sq miles) in area. The obvious jokes are made about it, but Mafia has no connection with Sicily and it is a safe and restful place to visit.

It has its own interesting history, and its relatively flat topography is not unattractive, but most visitors come to Mafia because of its beaches and its excellent reputation as a centre for sea-fishing, snorkelling and diving. Tanzania's first **marine park** is likely to be established here soon.

Below: *The technology of scuba diving mixes with the timelessness of an old dhow off the coast of Zanzibar.*

Zanzibar and Pemba at a Glance

On Zanzibar, Pemba and Mafia the best months in terms of weather are undoubtedly between **mid-May** and **mid-October**. January to March can be uncomfortably hot, although monsoon breezes often temper the sultry air. Rain in March and April, and to a lesser extent from mid-October to mid-December, can sometimes be heavy and frustrating.

The largest aircraft are unable to land on Zanzibar, so most visitors **fly** to Dar es Salaam, Nairobi or Mombasa. Air Tanzania has regular flights from Dar, and there are air charter services available. Flying time between Dar and Zanzibar is approx. 20 minutes.
Several **ferry** companies offer regular and speedy services to Zanzibar by hydrofoil, leaving from the customs jetty in Dar harbour. The ferries and their schedules are usually listed in the *Daily News* or the *Sunday News*.

The Stone Town should be explored on **foot**, if possible. Guides are not necessary but more experienced ones are usually available through your hotel or a travel agent. There are **taxis** and **car hire** available. Hotels can advise on special trips.

Guesthouses and some high-quality hotels are springing up quickly in Zanzibar as the tourist boom takes hold. Independent travellers should check with travel agents before leaving Dar.

Zanzibar Stone Town
Mazson's, tel: (054) 33694, fax: (054) 33695. One of the oldest houses in Shangani, the most interesting quarter of Zanzibar. Meals by room service; 40 rooms. Very pleasant.
Dhow Palace, tel: (054) 33012, fax: (054) 33008. Attractive 19th-century building in Shangani, typically Zanzibari in style and furnishings and carefully restored.
Emerson's House, tel: (054) 30609/32153, fax: (054) 33135. Keeps faith with true Zanzibari traditions. Self-contained rooms with air-conditioning and a reasonable restaurant.
Mbweni Ruins, tel: (054) 31832, fax: (054) 30536. Stylish little hotel with Victorian Zanzibar charm. Rooms have verandas overlooking Indian Ocean. Thatched restaurant and bar set on cliff by the sea.
Tembo Hotel, tel: (054) 33005, fax: (054) 33777. Early 19th-century building which was once the American consulate. Furnished in traditional Zanzibar style. Restaurant overlooking the sea serves simple but reasonable cuisine.

More moderately priced hotels (some of considerable architectural and historical interest) include **Africa House**, **Clove**, **International**, **Narrow Street**, the **Spice Inn** and the **Zanzibar Hotel**. They are all clean and comfortable, if a little unsophisticated in comparison to others on the island.

Beach Hotels, West Coast
Mawimbini Club Village, tel: (054) 31163. Luxury resort 16km (10 miles) north of Zanzibar Town with 32 bungalows furnished in Zanzibar style and with ceiling fans. Restaurant and bar, swimming pool, various water sports.
Mtoni Marine Centre, tel: (054) 32540, fax: (054) 25554. Located by a pleasant beach 3km (1 mile) north of Zanzibar Town. Activities include water sports, cruises, big game fishing and diving.
Reef Hotel, tel: (057) 30208, fax: (057) 30556. Large beach resort by Mbweni Beach, a short drive from Zanzibar airport. Attractive cluster of thatched chalets with all the facilities (including swimming pool) normally associated with an expensive resort.
Zanzibar Serena, contact Serena Central Reservations, Arusha, tel: (057) 8175/6304, fax: (057) 8282. Zanzibar's most luxurious hotel in terms of facilities and quality. Lovely situation by the sea on Shangani Point Restaurant, swimming pool, 52 rooms.

Zanzibar and Pemba at a Glance

Beach Hotels, East Coast

Matemwe Bungalows, tel: (057) 31342. a dozen huts situated on low cliffs overlooking a pleasant beach.
Mnemba Club, contact Coastal Travels. Situated on the tiny private island of Mnemba, 10 minutes from the Zanzibar mainland. Island surrounded by virgin reefs rich in fish and corals and by a beautiful beach. Ten tastefully built cottages, each with large veranda. Very good Italian food, all water sports. Closed April, May and June.
Tamarind Beach Hotel, tel: (054) 31859, fax: (054) 31859. Simple but pleasant hotel on mile-long beach at Uroa Bay.

Pemba

Pemba has hardly begun to realize its potential, and Chake Chake's **Hoteli ya Chake**, as its name suggests, makes few concessions to the demanding foreigner.

Mafia Island

Kinasi Camp, contact Coastal Travels. A small luxury camp (20 guests only) with an emphasis on 'stylish informality'. Activities focus upon diving, snorkelling, big game fishing, sailing, windsurfing, bird watching and picnic excursions. Also boasts excellent cuisine.
Mafia Island Lodge, contact (051) 27671. Rising reputation after extensive renovation.

WHERE TO EAT

Restaurants, like hotels, are opening up in Zanzibar all the time. Restaurants on Zanzibar are characterized by informality and friendliness rather than by famous reputations. However, some of the better ones include:
Sinbad Sailor's: Has established a good reputation.
The Fisherman's: French cuisine, seafood a speciality. Good value.
Sea View: Popular first-floor Indian restaurant overlooking the sea front, close to the former Sultan's Palace.

TOURS AND EXCURSIONS

Guided walking tours of the old Stone Town: 2 to 4 hours is usually adequate.
Spice Tours: Popular trips to the spice-growing areas to the north of Zanzibar town; organized by specialist companies such as Mitu's. The trip takes 4–5 hours.
Day trip to Jozani Forest: To see the rare red colobus monkeys. Can be combined with an afternoon on one of the beautiful east coast beaches.
Boat trips to Prison Island and/or **Grave Island:** Can be arranged through your hotel.

Alternatively, go down to the little beach just to the northeast of the Sultan's Palace in Stone Town, where you will usually find fishermen with a small boat or dhows willing to take you across.

USEFUL TELEPHONE NOS

Zanzibar code: 054.
Pemba code: 054.
Coastal Travels (Tours and Air charter): tel: (051) 37479/80, fax: (051) 46045.
Equator Tours, Zanzibar: tel: (054) 33799, fax: (054) 33882.
Hit Holidays: tel: (054) 33615/33660, fax: (054) 44055.
Kearsley Travel and Tours: tel: (051) 20607/8/9, fax: (051) 29085.
Savannah Tours: tel: (051) 25752/25237, fax: (051) 44568.
Selous Safari Co: tel: (051) 34802/28485, fax: (051) 46980.
Zanzibar Commission for Tourism (promotions): tel: (054) 33485/7, fax: (057) 8256.
Zanzibar Tourist Corporation (tours and info.): tel: (054) 32344.
The Zanzibar Dive Centre: tel: (054) 33686, fax: (054) 31342.

ZANZIBAR	J	F	M	A	M	J	J	A	S	O	N	D
AVERAGE TEMP. °F	81	81	81	79	79	77	75	75	77	77	79	81
AVERAGE TEMP. °C	27	27	27	26	26	25	24	24	25	25	26	27
HOURS OF SUN DAILY	8	8	7	5	6	8	7	8	8	8	8	8
RAINFALL ins.	3	3	5	15	10	2	2	2	2	3	9	6
RAINFALL mm	78	66	138	386	249	62	45	43	51	88	220	158
DAYS OF RAINFALL	7	6	12	19	14	4	5	6	6	7	14	12

Travel Tips

Tourist Information

The Tanzania Tourist Board has offices in Germany, Italy, Saudi Arabia, Sweden, UK and the USA.

In Tanzania its offices are in Dar es Salaam, PO Box 2485, tel: (051) 2761/4, fax: (051) 46780 and Arusha, PO Box 2348, tel: (057) 3842/3, fax: (057) 8256. The Zanzibar Commission for Tourism is in Zanzibar Town, PO Box 1410, tel: (054) 33485/7, fax: (054) 33448.

The Tanzanian National Parks Authority is based on the 6th floor, Kilimanjaro Wing, Arusha International Conference Centre, PO Box 3134, tel: (057) 3471/3181.

Entry Requirements

All visitors require a valid passport. Visas are required by everyone except:
• Nationals of Denmark, Ireland and the UK. All other EU nationals do require a visa.
• Nationals of Finland, Iceland, Kenya, Norway, Singapore, Sweden, Zimbabwe, most Caribbean states and a number of Indian Ocean and Pacific Ocean states.

• Holders of a Tanzania re-entry pass.

Under new regulations, visas can now be acquired on entry into Tanzania, but confirm this with your nearest Tanzanian diplomatic mission well before you leave.

Customs

Each visitor may import duty-free spirits (including liquors) or wine up to one litre; perfume and toilet water up to 250ml; and 200 cigarettes or 50 cigars or 250g of tobacco. Visitors buying local handicrafts should keep cash sales receipts in case they are asked for on departure.

Health Requirements

At present health control requires a valid yellow fever certificate for those passengers arriving from South America, Central Africa, West Africa and East Africa.

Cholera certificates are not required, but intending visitors are advised to consult their doctors well before travelling and to consider vaccinations for cholera, tetanus, hepatitis, TAB and polio.

Getting There

By Air: Dar es Salaam, Kilimanjaro Airport (between Arusha and Moshi) and Zanzibar are the main entry points by air. Nairobi, in neighbouring Kenya, provides connections to most parts of the world. Travellers leaving Tanzania by air (even from the mainland to Zanzibar) are required to pay US$20 airport tax in hard currency (*not* Tanzanian shillings).
By Road: Overland routes into Tanzania from Kenya include Nairobi to Arusha (border town Namanga); Nairobi/Mombasa to Moshi (border towns Taveta/Himo); and Mombasa to Tanga (border town Lungalunga). There is a border crossing between Zambia and Tanzania at Tunduma.

What to Pack

Lightweight clothing in neutral colours is best in the bush. Long-sleeved shirts and trousers help prevent the mosquitoes biting, and hats, sunglasses and comfortable shoes might make life easier and healthier when walking or camping. In the rains an umbrella or light raincoat might be handy. Light woollens are sometimes needed in the dry season evenings (mid-May to mid-October), and heavier clothing at altitude. Those climbing Kilimanjaro will need layers of warm and waterproof clothing. Strong and comfortable footwear is also needed at the higher altitudes. Evening or city clothes tend to be casual or smart/casual throughout Tanzania.

A **camera** with at least one long lens (200mm or above) is essential for good wildlife photographs, together with a good supply of film; a good pair of **binoculars** (the highest magnification is not always the best factor, and 7 or 8 X 50 is adequate); if you intend to go walking or camping, you might find a small **rucksack** with a torch, penknife and portable water bottle or flask very handy. Those who carry video cameras should bring a good supply of cassettes.

Money Matters

Currency: Tanzania operates a decimal system based on the Tanzanian shilling (TShs). Notes are in denominations of 50, 100, 200, 500 and 1000, 5000 and 10,000 TShs.
Exchange: Foreign currency (cash as well as travellers cheques) may be exchanged at bureaux de change or the larger hotels, although rates in hotels tend to be less favourable. Banks will also change money, but you might have to wait longer than you would in a bureau. The black

USEFUL PHRASES	
ENGLISH	**SWAHILI**
Hello	*Jambo*
How are you?	*Habari?*
Fine/OK	*Mzuri*
Thank you (very much)	
	Asante
	(sana)
Welcome!	*Karibu!*
	(pl. *Karibuni*)
Excuse me	*Samahani*
Goodbye	*Kwaheri*
Yes	*Ndiyo*
No	*Hapana*
Today	*Leo*
Tomorrow	*Kesho*
Hot	*Moto*
Cold	*Baridi*
Hotel	*Hoteli*
Room	*Chumba*
Bed	*Kitanda*
Shop	*Duka*
One	*Moja*
Two	*Mbili*
Three	*Tatu*
Four	*Ine*
Five	*Tano*

market has declined considerably in recent years but visitors can still expect to be approached by touts in the city streets – they should be politely turned away.
Banks: The main banks are: National Bank of Commerce Trust Bank; City Bank; First Adili Bank; Standbic Tanzania Ltd (South African registered) and Barclays (opening soon). Banking hours are: 08:30–12:30 and 13:00–1600 Mon–Fri; 08:30–11:30 Sat; 09:00–11:30 Sun.
Credit cards: Mastercard, American Express and Visa have only limited acceptance at present and visitors should not be dependent upon using them.

Tipping: Tipping for good service (approx 10%) is always appreciated. A service charge might be included in the bill, but whether this always reaches the appropriate pockets is questionable.

Accommodation

Hotels are graded by a star system (one to five), though these can often be misleading. There are a few hotels of the highest standard, with others being built. Below this there is a broad range of more moderately priced hotels. Low-budget hotels are plentiful and usually quite basic.

Some of the best accommodation is to be found in the national parks and reserves.

Transport

Road: Recent rehabilitation of roads has much improved the Tanzanian network. The tarmac highways between Zambia and Dar es Salaam (the Tanzam highway), and Dar and the north are both in good condition for most of their length. Elsewhere roads vary from good gravel or dirt tracks to potholed or corrugated trials of endurance. The situation is improving, and travellers should seek local information before travelling.
Petrol and diesel are usually available along the major tourist routes and in the towns. Independent travellers into the more remote regions or game parks must be self-sufficient in terms of fuel.

In the event of **breakdowns** on the open road, and if you do not have any warning signs, follow the local practice of spreading some leafy branches on the road behind and in front of your vehicle. If you cannot fix the vehicle yourself, wave down a passing traveller (expatriates and Asians are more likely to speak good English, but many long-distance truck drivers can be very helpful). With locals, discuss payment before accepting help or a tow. Local villagers will often gather around to stare – this can be unnerving or irritating, but is usually nothing but curiosity.

There are **garages** in all the large towns. Many of the mechanics are not very thoroughly trained so stay with your vehicle while it is being repaired and make sure you agree on an estimated price before repairs begin.

If you intend driving to remote parts of a particular game park, take a guide or notify the ranger or the manager of your lodge or camp. Familiarize yourself with the vehicle and general procedures on avoiding problems driving off-road. **Car hire** is expensive, but there are now more options with well-known firms such as Herz, Avis and Europcar operating in Dar and Arusha.

Visitors may drive in Tanzania using a valid international driving licence, which should be carried at all times when driving.

Driving is on the left. The speed limit on open roads is 110kph (70mph), except where indicated, and in towns 50kph (30mph).

Bus: Travelling locally on Tanzania's crowded bus services is not advised – it is better to pay for a taxi. Long-distance buses, however, have improved enormously in recent years, and the best of them are reasonably comfortable and air-conditioned. Routes covered include Dar to Moshi, Tanga to Moshi and Moshi to Arusha. Bus services to Nairobi and Mombasa are also available. Departure times of the main services are usually published in the local press.

Train: There are three major railway lines in Tanzania: Dar–Tanga–Moshi, Dar–Mwanza/Kigoma/ Mpanda and Dar–Mbeya–Zambia. Rail travel in Tanzania can be long, uncomfortable and tiring (the journey from Dar to Mwanza, for example, takes two days). The 'Uhuru' railway between Dar and Zambia is still the most reliable and comfortable of Tanzanian's railways, but services are deteriorating and first-class travel is advised.

Ferry: The fastest services between Dar and Zanzibar (taking just over one hour)

are the hydrofoils run by companies such as Sea Express, Flying Horse and Azam Marine, all of which are based at the customs jetty opposite St Joseph's Cathedral on the main Dar es Salaam seafront.

On Lake Victoria services run between Mwanza and Bukoba (in Tanzania), and Port Bell in Uganda.

The historical steamer, *M.V. Liemba*, still operates out of Kigoma on Lake Tanganyika, serving Zambia and Burundi.

Air: These operate between the larger towns and to Zanzibar. Overbooking and delays are sometimes a problem, but Air Tanzania is slowly improving.

Travelling with a local Safari Company

Tours of Tanzania and its main sights can be arranged locally, or through overseas agents, via one of many safari companies operating in Tanzania. Some of these are better than others, but remember that even the best have problems in a country where little is guaranteed. The companies which enjoy

CONVERSION CHART		
FROM	**TO**	**MULTIPLY BY**
Millimetres	Inches	0.0394
Metres	Yards	1.0936
Metres	Feet	3.281
Kilometres	Miles	0.6214
Kilometres square	Square miles	0.386
Hectares	Acres	2.471
Litres	Pints	1.760
Kilograms	Pounds	2.205
Tonnes	Tons	0.984
To convert Celsius to Fahrenheit: x 9 ÷ 5 + 32		

a good reputation at present include Abercrombie and Kent, Ker and Downey, Wildersun, Ranger and UCT. Other recommended companies in Arusha include Hoopoe Adventure Tours, Leopard Tours, Savannah Tours and Simba Safaris. There are others offering good value for money and visitors should shop around.

Before finalizing a deal, confirm the main points of the agreement in writing, which should include the number of people in your group, which places you will visit and for how long, where you will stay, meals, game drives included, and whether certian fees, such as those for the game parks, driver's allowance and tips, are included. Also determine what happens in the event of a serious breakdown or accident involving injuries to clients.

Business Hours
As a general rule shops open by about 09:00 and close by about 17:00, with a break for lunch from 12:00 until about 14:00. Small *dukas* selling groceries and general goods often stay open until late in the evening.

Time Difference
Tanzania has only one time zone, 3 hours ahead of GMT.

Communications
The Tanzanian telephone system is presently undergoing a long-awaited overhaul. There are effective public phones in Bridge St in Dar es Salaam, and reasonable phone lines in

---

PUBLIC HOLIDAYS

1 January •
New Year's Day
12 January •
Zanzibar Revolution Day
March/April • Good Friday
and Easter Monday
26 April • Union Day
1 May • International
Worker's Day
8 August •
Peasant's Day
9 December •
Independence Day
25 December •
Christmas Day

Holidays with variable dates:
Maulid • Celebrates birth
of the Prophet Mohammed
Idd ul Fitr • End of the Holy
Month of Ramadan
Idd el Haj • Celebrates
the sacrifice of Ismail and
is the time for the main
pilgrimage to Mecca.

---

the larger hotels (though a high commission is sometimes charged). Some of the lodges in the more popular parks have direct dialling facilities.

Electricity
The power system is 220/230 volts AC. US appliances require an adaptor. Plugs are usually 13-amp square pin. Power cuts are common, though most standard tourist hotels and lodges have their own generator.

Weights and Measures
Tanzania operates the metric system.

Health Precautions
Malaria is endemic in all lowland areas below 800m

(2600ft) and particularly virulent. Visitors should take prophylactics as prescribed by their doctor. A course of these should begin at least one week before entering the country, and carry on throughout and for two weeks after the stay. In the unlikely event of visitors experiencing any kind of fever on their return home they *must* seek treatment immediately and inform their doctor of the possiblity of malaria. Measures which can be taken to prevent malaria also include the use of mosquito nets at night, spraying of rooms with insecticide, the application of insect repellant and the wearing of long-sleeved shirts, long trousers, socks and so on in the evenings and early mornings.

Other insect-borne diseases such as **yellow fever** and **sleeping sickness** are present, but for visitors there is little actual fear of contacting most of them. Tsetse flies, one species of which carries sleeping sickness, can give travellers in the bush a sharp little bite, but very few victims actually suffer anything worse than this.

Bilharzia is a debilitating water-borne disease, caused by a parasitical worm, which can easily be caught by swimming in certain lakes, pools and rivers. Lake Victoria is heavily infested. The disease is easily avoided, by resisting any temptation to swim or wash in such waters.

AIDS is now widespread in Tanzania.

Tanzania, especially during and just after the rains, is full of **creepy crawlies**. Few are threatening, but common sense should be employed. Scorpion, snake and spider bites are very rare and even then seldom fatal.

On the coast, spiny sea-urchins and stone-fish can cause problems, but they are seldom encountered by tourists. If in doubt, wear strong and thick-soled canvas shoes, and ask for advice at your hotel.

Try to avoid untreated **water**, ice-cubes and raw vegetables, and peel all fruit. Tap water is unsafe for drinking or brushing teeth. Mineral water is available in the larger towns and many restaurants, and most hotels and lodges usually provide flasks of boiled and filtered water (not always to be trusted). Independent travellers should boil or sterilize drinking water and milk.

Cuts, **bites** and **stings** are liable to turn septic if left untreated, so an appropriate ointment should be applied as soon as possible. Cuts and grazes from coral can be particularly easily infected.

Health Services

There are qualified doctors on hand in the major towns, as well as pharmacies selling a wide range of medicines. In the more popular parks many lodges and camps have qualified doctors on hand or on radio call, and in the unlikely event of major accidents or serious illness,

patients would be flown out, usually fairly quickly, to an appropriate hospital. Similarly, walkers and climbers on Kilimanjaro can expect fairly efficient medical evacuation in the event of an emergency.

Most travel companies insist on their clients taking out **medical insurance**, but if this is not the case, travellers should make sure that they insure their health before their trip begins.

Security

Petty thieving, thefts of and from cars and more serious robberies are on the increase in Tanzania, as they are elsewhere. Care should always be taken of personal property, especially attractive items such as money, jewellery, cameras etc. Don't advertize your relative wealth and be careful, even when in a car, of wearing jewellery as such items as watches and necklaces are sometimes snatched through open windows when the car is stopped. Similarly, beware of pickpockets in crowded places, and con-men who suddenly 'recognize' you from the airport. In the unlikely event of more serious robberies, do not resist.

Drug-related problems, including addiction itself, are also on the increase, though again, you are unlikely to encounter unpleasant incidents.

Emergencies

Contact the nearest police station or dial 999.

Etiquette

Visitors often feel uncomfortable haggling. In most shopping situations it is acceptable and necessary, especially when buying souvenirs. Some shops, however, such as supermarkets and chemists, have fixed prices.

Language

The national language is Kiswahili, though English is widely spoken in most areas popular with tourists (see p. 123).

GOOD READING

Boyd, William (1983) *An Ice Cream War* (Penguin).
Goodall, Jane (1971) *In the Shadow of Man* (Collins).
Goodall, Jane (1990) *Through a Window* (Wiedenfield and Nicholson).
Grzimek, B. (1959) *Serengeti Shall Not Die* (Collins).
Packenham, T. (1991) *The Scramble for Africa* (Wiedenfield and Nicholson).
Useful field guides are *Field Guide to the Birds of East Africa,* and *Field Guide to the National Parks of East Africa,* both by John Williams (both Collins).
A series of small but useful guides to the various national parks are available in some hotels, lodges and bookshops, or at park entrance gates.
If you intend to walk or climb to the summit of Kilimanjaro, look at Iain Allan's *Guide to Mount Kenya and Kilimanjaro* (Mountain Club of Kenya).

INDEX